THE SCIENCE OF GETTING RICH

AND

THE ART OF MONEY GETTING

by
Wallace D. Wattles
P. T. Barnum

CLASSY
PUBLISHING

THE SCIENCE OF GETTING RICH AND THE ART OF MONEY GETTING
Wallace D. Wattles & P. T. Barnum
Published by Classy Publishing, 2024

www.classypublishing.com
info@classypublishing.com

ISBN: 978-93-5522-914-4

No part of this publication may be reproduced, stored in a retrieval system,
or transmitted, in any form or by any means, electronic, mechanical, photocopying,
recording or otherwise, without the prior permission of the publisher.

Cover Design by Classy Publishing

CONTENTS

THE SCIENCE OF GETTING RICH

Preface		3
1.	The Right to be Rich	5
2.	There Is a Science of Getting Rich	8
3.	Is Opportunity Monopolized?	11
4.	The First Principle	14
5.	Increasing Life	19
6.	How Riches Come to You	24
7.	Gratitude	28
8.	Thinking in the Certain Way	32
9.	How to Use the Will	36
10.	Further Use of the Will	40
11.	Acting in the Certain Way	45
12.	Efficient Action	50
13.	Getting into the Right Business	54
14.	The Impression of Increase	58
15.	The Advancing Man	62
16.	Cautions and Concluding Observations	66
17.	A Summary of the Science of Getting Rich	70
Questions		72

THE ART OF MONEY GETTING

Introduction	79
Don't Mistake Your Vocation	88
Select the Right Location	90
Avoid Debt	92
Persevere	95

Whatever You Do, Do It with All Your Might	97
Use the Best Tools	100
Don't Get Above Your Business	102
Learn Something Useful	106
Let Hope Predominate, but be not Too Visionary	107
Do not Scatter Your Powers	108
Be Systematic	109
Read the Newspapers	111
Beware of "Outside Operations"	112
Don't Indorse without Security	114
Advertise Your Business	116
"Don't Read the Other Side"	119
Be Polite and Kind to Your Customers	121
Be Charitable	123
Don't Blab	124
Preserve Your Integrity	125

THE SCIENCE OF GETTING RICH

Wallace D. Wattles

Preface

This book is pragmatical, not philosophical. It is a practical manual, not a treatise on theories. It is intended for the men and women whose most pressing need is for money—for people who wish to get rich first and philosophize afterward. It is for those who have, so far, found neither the time, the means, or the opportunity to go deeply into the study of metaphysics. It is intended for those who want results and who are willing to take the conclusions of science as a basis for action—without going into all the processes by which those conclusions were reached.

I expect the reader to take my statements on faith just as he would take statements concerning a law of electrical action if they were promulgated by a Marconi or an Edison. By taking these statements on faith, he will prove their truth by acting upon them without fear or hesitation. Every man or woman who does this will certainly get rich. The science in this book is an exact science, and failure is impossible. Nevertheless, for the benefit of those who wish to investigate philosophical theories and so secure a logical basis for faith, I will cite certain authorities.

The monistic theory of the universe—the theory that one substance appears to manifest itself as the many elements of the material world—is of Hindu origin and has been gradually winning its way into the thought of the Western world for two hundred years. It is the foundation of all the Oriental philosophies and has found a place in the thought of Descartes, Spinoza, Leibnitz, Schopenhauer, Hegel, and Emerson. The reader who would dig to the philosophical foundations is advised to read Hegel and Emerson for himself.

In writing this book I have used a plain style so that all might understand. The following plan of action has been thoroughly tested and bears the supreme test for any practical experiment: it works. If you wish to know how the conclusions were arrived at, read the writings of the authors mentioned above. If you wish to reap the fruits of their philosophies in actual practice, read this book and do exactly as it tells you to do.

Wallace D Wattles

CHAPTER 1

The Right to be Rich

Whatever may be said in praise of poverty, the fact remains that it is not possible to live a really complete or successful life unless one is rich. No person can rise to his greatest possible height in talent or soul development unless he has plenty of money. In order to unfold the soul and to develop talent he must have many things to use, and he cannot have these things unless he has money to buy them with.

People develop in mind, soul, and body by making use of things, and society is so organized that people must have money in order to become the possessor of things. Therefore, the basis of all human advancement must be the science of getting rich.

The object of all life is development. Everything that lives has an inalienable right to all the development it is capable of attaining.

A person's right to life means his right to have the free and unrestricted use of all the things which may be necessary to his fullest mental, spiritual, and physical unfolding—in other words, his right to be rich.

In this book, I shall not speak of riches in a figurative way. To be really rich does not mean to be satisfied or contented with a little. No person ought to be satisfied with a little if he is capable of using and enjoying more. The purpose of nature is the advancement and development of life. Every individual should have all that can contribute to the power, elegance, beauty, and richness of life.

The person who owns all he wants for the living of all the life he is capable of living is rich. Nobody can have all he wants without plenty of money. Life has advanced so far and become so complex that even the most ordinary man or woman requires a great amount of wealth in order to live in a manner that even approaches completeness. Every person naturally wants to become all that he is capable of becoming; this desire to realize innate possibilities is inherent in human nature. Success in life is becoming what you want to be. You can become what you want to be only by making use of things, and you can have the free use of things only as you become rich enough to buy them. Therefore, an understanding of the science of getting rich is the most essential of all knowledge.

There is nothing wrong in wanting to get rich. The desire for riches is really the desire for a richer, fuller, and more abundant life. And, that desire is praiseworthy. The person who does not desire to live more abundantly is uncommon. And the individual who does not desire to have money enough to buy all he wants may not be living to his full potential.

There are three motives for which we live: we live for the body, the mind, and the soul. No one of these is better or holier than the other. Each is desirable, and neither body, mind, or soul can live fully if one of the others is cut short of full life and expression. It is not right or noble to live only for the soul and deny mind or body. It is wrong to live for the intellect and deny body and soul.

We are all acquainted with the loathsome consequences of living for the body and denying both mind and soul. We see that real life means the complete expression of all that a person can give forth through body, mind, and soul. No person can be really happy or satisfied unless his body is living fully in every function and unless the same is true of his mind and his soul. Wherever there is an unexpressed possibility or an unperformed function, there is an unsatisfied desire. Desire is possibility seeking expression or function seeking performance.

A person cannot live fully in body without good food, comfortable clothing, warm shelter, and freedom from excessive toil. Rest and recreation are also necessary to his physical life.

He cannot live fully in mind without books and time to study them, without opportunity for travel and observation, or without intellectual companionship. To live fully in mind he must have intellectual recreations and must surround himself with all the objects of art and beauty he is capable of using and appreciating.

To live fully in soul, an individual must have love. And the expression of love is often frustrated by poverty.

An individual's highest happiness is found in the bestowal of benefits on those he loves. Love finds its most natural and spontaneous expression in giving. The person who has nothing to give cannot fill his place as a husband or father, as a citizen, or as a human being. It is in the use of material things, that a person finds full life for his body, develops his mind, and unfolds his soul. It is therefore of supreme importance to be rich.

It is perfectly right that you should desire to be rich. If you are a normal man or woman you cannot help doing so. It is perfectly right that you should give your best attention to the science of getting rich because it is the noblest and most necessary of all studies. If you neglect this study, you are derelict in your duty to yourself, to God, and to humanity. You can render God and humanity no greater service than to make the most of yourself.

CHAPTER 2

There Is a Science of Getting Rich

There is a science of getting rich. It is an exact science, like algebra or arithmetic. There are certain laws which govern the process of acquiring riches. Once a person learns and obeys these laws, he will get rich with mathematical certainty.

The ownership of money and property comes as a result of doing things in a certain way. Those who do things in this certain way, whether on purpose or accidentally, get rich. Those who do not do things in this certain way, no matter how hard they work or how able they are, remain poor.

It is a natural law that like causes always produce like effects. Therefore, any man or woman who learns to do things in this certain way will infallibly get rich.

That the above statement is true is shown by the following facts.

Getting rich is not a matter of environment. If it were, all the people in certain areas would become wealthy. The people of one city would all be rich, while those of other towns would all be poor. The inhabitants of one state would roll in wealth, while those of an adjoining state would be in poverty.

We frequently see rich and poor living in the same environment and often engaged in the same vocations. When two people are in the same locality and in the same business—and one gets rich while the other remains poor—it shows that getting rich is not primarily a matter of environment. Some environments may be more favorable than others, but when two people in the same business are in the same neighborhood—and one gets rich while the other fails—it indicates that getting rich is the result of doing things in a certain way.

And, furthermore, the ability to do things in this certain way is not due solely to the possession of talent, because many people who have great talent remain poor, while others who have very little talent get rich.

If we study people who have gotten rich, we find that they are an average lot in all respects. It is evident that they do not get rich because they possess unique talents and abilities. They get rich because they happen to do things in a certain way.

Getting rich is not the result of saving or thrift. Many very penurious people are poor, while free spenders often get rich.

Nor is getting rich due to doing things which others fail to do. Two people in the same business often do almost exactly the same things, and one gets rich while the other remains poor or becomes bankrupt.

From all these things, we must come to the conclusion that getting rich is the result of doing things in a certain way.

If getting rich is the result of doing things in a certain way, then any man or woman who can do things in that way can become rich. And if like causes always produce like effects, the whole matter can be brought within the domain of an exact science.

The question arises whether this certain way may not be so difficult that only a few may follow it. As we have seen, this cannot be true so far as natural ability is concerned. Talented people get rich, and blockheads get rich. Intellectually brilliant people get rich, and very stupid people get rich. Physically strong people get rich, and weak and sickly people get rich.

Some degree of ability to think and understand is, of course, essential. But, in so far as natural ability is concerned, any man or woman who has sense enough to read and understand these words can certainly get rich.

Although we have seen that it is not a matter of environment, location does count for something. One would not go to the heart of the Sahara and expect to do successful business.

Getting rich involves the necessity of dealing with people and of being where there are people to deal with. But, that is about as far as environment matters. If anybody else in your town can get rich, so can you. If anybody else in your state can get rich, so can you.

Again, it is not a matter of choosing some particular business or profession. People get rich in every business and in every profession—while their next door neighbors in the same vocation remain in poverty.

It is true that you will do best in a business which you like. And, if you have certain talents which are well developed, you will do best in a business which calls for the exercise of those talents.

Also, you will do best in a business which is suited to your locality. An ice cream parlor would do better in a warm climate than in Greenland. A salmon fishery will succeed better in the Northwest than in Florida where there are no salmon.

But, aside from these general limitations, getting rich is not dependent on your engaging in some particular business, but on your learning to do things in a certain way. If you are now in business—and someone else in your locality is getting rich in the same business, while you are not getting rich—it is because you are not doing things in the same way that the other person is doing them.

No one is prevented from getting rich by lack of capital. True, as you get capital, its increase becomes more easy and rapid. But, no matter how poor you may be—if you begin to do things in a certain way—you will begin to have capital. The getting of capital is a part of the process of getting rich. It is a part of the result which invariably follows the doing of things in a certain way.

You may be the poorest person on the continent and be deeply in debt, but if you begin to do things in this certain way, you must infallibly begin to get rich. Because like causes must produce like effects, you will get rich even if you do not have any friends, influence, or other resources. If you have no capital, you can get capital. If you are in the wrong business, you can get into the right business. If you are in the wrong location, you can go to the right location. You can do so by beginning in your present business and in your present location to do things in a certain way which causes success.

CHAPTER 3

Is Opportunity Monopolized?

No person is kept poor because opportunity has been taken away from him—because other people have monopolized the wealth and have put a fence around it. You may decide not to engage in certain kinds of business, but there are other channels open to you. It would probably be hard for you to get control of any of the great fuel and power generating companies. But, alternative energy forms—such as solar energy and electricity produced through wind and other natural forces—are businesses that are still in their infancy and that have great potential. It will be only a few years until there are new systems of communication and transportation (electrical cars, space travel, microwave transmission, etc.) in very different forms than now envisioned. These will develop into great industries which will give employment to hundreds of thousands, perhaps millions, of people. Why not turn your attention to the development of these businesses, instead of competing with the big conglomerates for a chance in the business world?

It is quite true that if you are a worker in the employ of a power producing plant, there is little chance of you becoming owner of the plant in which you work. But, it is also true that if you begin to act in a certain way, you can soon leave the employ of the power company, buy a farm of from ten to forty acres, and engage in business as a producer of natural foodstuffs and organic products. Or, you can go into hydroponic cultivation (the growing of plants in nutrient solutions) which produces high yields in small areas. There is presently a great opportunity for men and women to organically cultivate small tracts of land. You may say that it is impossible for you to get the land, but I am going to prove to you that it is not impossible—that you can certainly get a farm if you will go to work in a certain way.

At different periods the tide of opportunity moves in different directions, according to the needs of the whole and to the particular stage of social evolution which has been reached. At present, in America, it is moving toward decentralization and toward industries that can be decentralized. Today, more opportunity is open to the organic and herbal farmer than to the office worker. More opportunity is open to the businessman who works in the field of new energy forms and ecologically sound endeavors than to the executive on the corporate treadmill.

There is an abundance of opportunity for the man who will go with the tide, instead of trying to swim against it.

Office workers, either as individuals or as a group, are not deprived of opportunity. The workers are not being kept down by their masters—by the powers of big business and the conglomerates. As a group, they are where they are because they do things in a certain way.

When it begins to do things in a certain way, the working class can become the master class. The law of wealth is the same for it as it is for all other groups. Workers will remain where they are as long as they continue to do as they do. The individual worker, however, is not held down by the ignorance or the mental slothfulness of his class; he can follow the tide of opportunity to riches. This book will tell him how.

No one is kept in poverty by a shortness in the supply of riches. There is more than enough for all. A palace as large as the capitol at Washington could be built for every family on earth from the building material available in the United States alone. Under intensive cultivation, this country could produce enough wool, cotton, linen, silk, and food to clothe and feed each person in the world. The visible supply is practically inexhaustible. And, the invisible supply really is inexhaustible.

Everything you see on earth is made from one original substance, out of which all things proceed. New forms are constantly being made and older ones are dissolving, but all are shapes assumed by one thing.

There is no limit to the supply of formless stuff or original substance. The universe is made out of it, but it was not all used in making the universe. The spaces in, through, and between the forms of the visible universe are permeated and filled with the original substance—with the formless stuff, with the raw material of all things. Ten thousand universes can still be made, and even then, the supply of universal raw material will not be exhausted.

No person, therefore, is poor because nature is poor or because there is not enough to go around.

Nature is an inexhaustible storehouse of riches. The supply will never run short. Original substance is alive with creative energy and is constantly producing more forms. When the supply of building material is exhausted, more will be produced. When the soil is exhausted so that foodstuffs and materials for clothing will no longer grow upon it, it will be renewed or more soil will be made. When all the gold and silver has been dug from the earth—if human beings are still in such a stage of social development as to need gold and silver—more will be produced from the formless. The formless stuff responds to the needs of humans; it will not let them be without any good thing.

This is true of man collectively. The race as a whole is always abundantly rich. If individuals are poor, it is because they do not follow a certain way of doing things which makes the individual man rich.

The formless stuff is intelligent; it is material which thinks. It is alive and is always impelled toward more life.

It is the natural and inherent impulse of life to seek to live more. It is the nature of intelligence to enlarge itself and the quality of consciousness to seek to extend its boundaries and find fuller expression. The universe of forms has been made by formless living substance, throwing itself into form in order to express itself more fully.

The universe is a great living presence, always moving inherently toward more life and fuller functioning.

Nature is formed for the advancement of life; its motive is the increase of life. For this reason, everything which can possibly minister to life is bountifully provided. There can be no lack unless God is to contradict himself and nullify his own works. You are not kept poor by a shortness in the supply of riches. I shall demonstrate a little farther on that even the resources of the formless supply are at the command of any man or woman who will act and think in a certain way.

CHAPTER 4

The First Principle

Thought is the only power which can produce tangible riches from the formless substance. The stuff from which all things are made is a substance which thinks. A thought of form in this substance produces the form.

Original substance moves according to its thoughts. Every form and process you see in nature is the visible expression of a thought in the original substance. As it thinks of a form, it takes that form; as it thinks of a motion, it makes that motion. That is the way all things were created. We live in a thought world, and this world is a part of a thought universe.

The thought of a moving universe extended through—out the formless substance. The thinking stuff resulting from that thought, took the form of systems of planets and continues to maintain that form. Thinking substance takes the form of its thought and moves according to the thought. Holding the idea of a circling system of suns and worlds, it took the form of these bodies, and moved them accordingly.

Although centuries may be required to do the work, by thinking the form of a slow growing tree, the formless substance produces the tree. In creating, the formless substance seems to move according to the lines of motion it has established. The thought of an oak tree does not cause the instant formation of a full grown tree, but it does start in motion the forces which will produce the tree along established lines of growth.

Every thought of form, held in thinking substance, causes the creation of that form—but always, or at least generally, along lines of growth and action already established.

If the thought of a house of a certain construction were impressed upon the formless substance, it might not cause the instant formation of that house. But, it would cause the turning of creative energies already working in trade and commerce into such channels as to result in the speedy building of the house. And, if there were no existing channels through which the creative energy could work, the house would be formed directly from primal substance—without waiting for the slow processes of the organic and inorganic world.

No thought of form can be impressed upon the original substance without causing the creation of that form.

A human being is a thinking center and can originate thought. All the forms that a person fashions with his hands must first emerge from his thought. He cannot shape a thing until he has thought that thing.

And, so far man has confined his efforts wholly to the work of his hands; he has applied manual labor to the world of forms—seeking to change or modify already existing forms. He has never thought of trying to cause the creation of new forms by impressing his thoughts upon the formless substance.

When a person has a thought form, he takes material from the forms of nature and makes an image of the form which is in his mind. He has, so far, made little or no effort to cooperate with the formless intelligence to work "with the Father." He has not dreamed that he can "do what he seeth the Father doing." Man reshapes and modifies existing forms by manual labor. He has not considered the question of whether he could produce things from the formless substance by communicating his thoughts to it. I propose to prove that he may do so, to prove that any man or woman may do so, and to show how. My first step will be to lay down three fundamental propositions.

First, we assert that there is one original formless substance from which all things are made. All the seemingly many elements are only different presentations of one element. All the many forms found in organic and inorganic nature are only different shapes made from the same stuff. And, this stuff is thinking stuff; a thought held in it produces the form of the thought. Thought, in thinking substance, produces shapes. A human being is a thinking center, capable of original thought. If a person can communicate his thought to original thinking substance, he can cause the creation or formation of the thing he thinks about. To summarize this:

> *There is a thinking stuff from which all things are made, and which, in its original state, permeates, penetrates, and fills the interspaces of the universe.*
>
> *A thought in this substance produces the thing that is imaged by the thought.*
>
> *A person can form things in his though t, and by impressing his thought upon form less substance, can cause the thing he thinks about to be created.*

I can prove these statements by both logic and experience. Reasoning back from the phenomena of form and thought, I come to one original thinking substance. And, reasoning forward from this thinking substance, I come to the individual's power to cause the formation of the thing he thinks about.

By experiment, I find this reasoning to be true, and this is my strongest proof. If one person who reads this book gets rich by doing what I tell him to do, that is evidence in support of my claim. Furthermore, if every person who does what I tell him to do gets rich, that is positive proof until someone goes through the process and fails. The theory is true until the process fails, and this process will not fail because every person who does exactly what I tell him to do will get rich.

I have said that an individual gets rich by doing things in a certain way. In order to do so, a person must become able to think in a certain way. A person's way of doing things is the direct result of the way he thinks about things.

To do things in a way you want to do them, you will have to acquire the ability to think the way you want to think. This is the first step toward getting rich. To think what you want to think is to think *truth*, regardless of appearances.

Every person has the natural and inherent power to think what he wants to think, but it requires far more effort to do so than it does to think the thoughts which are suggested by appearances. To think according to appearances is easy. To think truth regardless of appearances is laborious and requires the expenditure of more power than any other work a person has to perform.

There is no labor from which most people shrink as they do from that of sustained and consecutive thought; it is the hardest work in the world. This is especially true when truth is contrary to appearances. Every appearance in the visible world tends to produce a corresponding form in the mind which observes it. This can only be prevented by holding the thought of the *truth*.

To look upon the appearance of disease will produce the form of disease in your own mind—and ultimately in your body. Instead, you must hold the thought of the *truth,* which is that there is no disease. Disease is only an appearance, and the reality is health.

To look upon the appearances of poverty will produce corresponding forms in your own mind. Instead, you must hold to the truth that there is no poverty. There is only abundance.

It requires power to think health when surrounded by the appearances of disease, or to think riches when in the midst of the appearances of poverty. But, he who acquires this power becomes a master mind. He can conquer fate; he can have what he wants.

This power can only be acquired by getting hold of the basic fact which is behind all appearances: that there is one thinking substance, from which and by which all things are made.

Then, we must grasp the truth that every thought held in this substance becomes a form and that a person can impress his thoughts upon it so as to cause them to take form and become visible things.

When we realize this, we lose all doubt and fear because we know that we can create what we want to create. We can get what we want to have and can become what we want to be. As a first step toward getting rich, you must believe the three fundamental statements given previously in this chapter. In order to emphasize them, I will repeat them here:

There is a thinking stuff from which all things are made, and which, in its original state, permeates, penetrates, and fills the interspaces of the universe.

A thought in this substance produces the thing that is imaged by the thought.

A person can form things in his though t, and by impressing his thought upon form less substance, can cause the thing he thinks about to be created.

You must lay aside all other concepts of the universe than this monistic one. You must dwell upon this until it is fixed in your mind and has become your habitual thought. Read these creed statements over and over again. Fix every word upon your memory, and meditate upon them until you firmly believe what they say. If a doubt comes to you, cast it aside as a sin.

Do not listen to arguments against this idea; do not go to churches or lectures where a contrary concept of things is taught or preached. Do not read magazines or books which teach a different idea. If you get mixed up in your faith, all your efforts will be in vain.

Do not ask why these things are true, nor speculate as to how they can be true. Simply take them on trust.

The science of getting rich begins with the absolute acceptance of this faith.

CHAPTER 5

Increasing Life

You must get rid of the last vestige of the old idea that there is a deity whose will it is that you should be poor or whose purposes may be served by keeping you in poverty.

The intelligent substance, which is everything and lives in everything, lives in you. It is a consciously living substance. Being a consciously living substance, it must have the natural and inherent desire of every living intelligence for the increase of life. Every living thing must continually seek for the enlargement of its life because life—in the mere act of living—must increase itself.

A seed, dropped into the ground, springs into activity, and in the act of living, produces a hundred more seeds. Life, by living, multiplies itself. It is forever becoming more; it must do so to continue to exist.

Intelligence is under this same necessity for continuous increase. Every thought we think makes it necessary for us to think another thought. Consciousness is continually expanding. Every fact we learn leads us to the learning of another fact. Knowledge is continually increasing. Every talent we cultivate brings to the mind the desire to cultivate another talent. We are subject to the urge of life. In seeking expression for this urge, we are impelled to know more, to do more, and to be more.

In order to know more, do more, and be more, we must have more. We must have things to use because we learn and do and become only by using things. We must get rich so that we can live more.

The desire for riches is simply the capacity for larger life seeking fulfillment; every desire is the effort of an unexpressed possibility to come into action. It is power seeking to manifest which causes desire. That which makes you want more money is the same as that which makes the plant grow. It is life, seeking fuller expression.

The one living substance must be subject to this law for all of life. It is permeated with the desire to live more; that is why it is under the necessity of creating things. Because this substance desires to live more in you, it wants you to have all the things you can use.

It is the desire of God that you should get rich. He wants you to get rich because he can express himself better through you if you have plenty of things to use in giving him expression. He can live more in you if you have unlimited command of the means of life.

The universe desires you to have everything you want to have. Nature is friendly to your plans. Everything is naturally for you. Make up your mind that this is true.

It is essential, however, that your purpose should harmonize with the purpose that is in everything.

You must want real life, not mere pleasure or sensual gratification. Life is the performance of function, and the individual really lives only when he performs without excess every function—physical, mental, and spiritual—of which he is capable.

You do not want to get rich in order to live swinishly for the gratification of animal desires. That is not life. But, the performance of every physical function is a part of life, and no one lives completely who denies the impulses of the body a normal and healthful expression.

You do not want to get rich solely to enjoy mental pleasures, to get knowledge, to gratify ambition, to outshine others, or to be famous. All these are a legitimate part of life; however, the person who only lives for the pleasures of the intellect alone will only have a partial life. He will never be satisfied with his lot.

You do not want to get rich solely for the good of others. Nor do you wish to lose yourself for the salvation of humanity or to only experience the joys of philanthropy and sacrifice. The joys of the soul are only a part of life. They are no better or nobler than any other part.

You want to get rich so that you can eat, drink, and be merry when it is time to do these things. You want to be rich so that you may surround yourself with beautiful things, see distant lands, feed your mind, and develop your intellect. You want to be rich so that you may love people, do kind things, and be able to play a good part in helping the world to find truth.

But, remember that extreme altruism is no better and no nobler than extreme selfishness. Both are mistakes.

Get rid of the idea that God wants you to sacrifice yourself for others, that you can secure his favor by doing so. God requires nothing of the kind.

What he wants is that you should make the most of yourself—for yourself, and for others. And, you can help others more by making the most of yourself than in any other way.

You can make the most of yourself only by getting rich. Thus, it is right and praiseworthy that you should give your first and best thought to the work of acquiring wealth.

Remember, however, that the desire of substance is for all. Its movements must be for more life to all; it cannot be made to work for less life to any because it is seeking riches and life in everything and in everyone.

The intelligent substance will make things for you, but it will not take things away from someone else and give them to you.

You must get rid of the thought of competition. You are to create, not to compete for what is already created. You do not have to take anything away from anyone. You do not have to drive sharp bargains. You do not have to cheat or to take advantage. You do not need to let any man work for you for less than he earns.

You do not have to covet the property of others or to look at it with wishful eyes. No one has anything of which you cannot have the same. And, you can have it without taking what he has away from him.

You are to become a creator, not a competitor. You are going to get what you want, but in such a way that when you get it every other person will have more than he has now.

I am aware that there are people who acquire a vast amount of money by proceeding in direct opposition to the directions in the preceding paragraph. Those of the plutocratic type, who become very rich, sometimes do so purely through their extraordinary ability on the plane of competition. However, sometimes—for example, in their contribution to the growth of industry—they unconsciously harmonize with substance in its movement toward the betterment of humanity. Rockefeller, Carnegie, Morgan, et al., have been the unconscious agents of the Supreme Power in the necessary work of systematizing and organizing productive industry. Their work has contributed immensely toward increased life for all. They helped to organize production and were soon succeeded by the agents of the multitude, who organized the machinery of distribution.

The multimillionaires are like the monster reptiles of prehistoric eras. They play a necessary part in the evolutionary process, but the same power which produced them will dispose of them. And, it is well to bear in mind that they have never been really rich. A record of the private lives of most of this class will show that they have really been the most abject and wretched of the poor.

Riches secured on the competitive plane are never satisfactory and permanent. They are yours today and another's tomorrow. Remember, if you are to become rich in a scientific and certain way, you must rise entirely out of competitive thought. You must never think for a moment that the supply is limited. You drop into the competitive mind the moment you begin to think that all the money is being "cornered" and controlled by bankers and others and that you must exert yourself to get laws passed to stop this process. Your power to cause creation will temporarily disappear, and what is worse, you will probably arrest the creative movements you have already instituted.

Know that there are countless millions of dollars' worth of undiscovered gold in the mountains of the earth. Know that if there were not, more would be created from the thinking substance to supply your needs. Know that the money you need will come—even if it is necessary for a thousand people to be led to the discovery of new gold mines tomorrow.

Never look at the visible supply; always look at the limitless riches in the formless substance and know that they are coming to you as fast as you can receive and use them. Nobody, by cornering the visible supply, can prevent you from getting what is yours.

Never allow yourself to think for an instant that all the best building spots will be taken before you get ready to build your house. Never worry about the trusts and combines and get anxious for fear they will soon come to own the whole earth. Never get afraid that you will lose what you want because some other person "beats you to it." That cannot possibly happen. You are not seeking anything that is possessed by anybody else; you are causing what you want to be created from the formless substance. And, the supply is limitless. Stick to the formulated statement:

> *There is a thinking stuff from which all things are made, and which, in its original state, permeates, penetrates, and fills the interspaces of the universe.*
>
> *A thought in this substance produces the thing that is imaged by the thought.*
>
> *A person can form things in his though t, and by impressing his thought upon form less substance, can cause the thing he thinks about to be created.*

CHAPTER 6

How Riches Come to You

When I say that you do not have to drive sharp bargains, I do not mean that you do not have to drive any bargains at all or that you are above the necessity for having any dealings with other people. I mean that you will not need to deal with them unfairly; you do not have to get something for nothing. You can give to every person more than you take from him.

You cannot give a person more in cash value than you take from him, but you can give him more in use value than the cash value of the thing you take from him. The paper, ink, and other material in this book may not be worth the money you paid for it. But, if the ideas in this book bring you thousands of dollars, you have not been wronged by those who sold it to you. They have given you a great use value for a small cash value.

Let us suppose that I own a picture which in any civilized community is worth thousands of dollars. I take it to Baffin Bay, and by "salesmanship" induce an Eskimo to give a bundle of furs worth $500 for it. I have really wronged him because he has no use for the picture. It has no use value to him; it will not add to his life.

But, suppose I give him a gun worth $50 for his furs. Then he has made a good bargain. He has use for the gun; it will get him more furs and much food; it will add to his life in every way; it will make him rich.

When you rise from the competitive to the creative plane, you can scan your business transactions very strictly. If you see that you are selling a person anything which does not add more to his life than the thing he gives you in exchange, you can afford to stop it. You do not have to beat anybody in business. And, if you are in a business which does beat people, get out of it at once.

Give every person more in use value than you take from him in cash value. Then, you are adding to the life of the world with every business transaction.

If you have people working for you, you must take from them more in cash value than you pay them in wages. But, you can organize your business so that it will be filled with the principle of advancement. Thus, each employee who wishes to do so may advance a little every day.

You can make your business do for your employees what this book is doing for you. You can conduct your business so that it will be a ladder by which every willing employee may climb to riches himself. And, it is not your fault if he does not accept the opportunity.

Even though you can cause your riches to come out of the formless substance which permeates all of your environment, it does not follow that your fortune will immediately take shape from the atmosphere and come into being before your eyes.

If you want a sewing machine, for instance, I would suggest that before you impress the thought of a sewing machine on the thinking substance, you first make sure the image of the machine is clearly formed in your mind. If you want a sewing machine, hold the mental image of it with the most positive certainty that it is being made or is on its way to you. After once forming the thought, have the most absolute and unquestioning faith that the sewing machine is coming. Never think of it or speak of it without feeling confident that it will arrive. Claim it as already yours.

It will be brought to you by the power of the supreme intelligence, acting upon the minds of men. If you live in Maine, it may be that a person will be brought from Texas or Japan to engage in some transaction which will result in your getting what you want. If so, the whole matter will be as much to that person's advantage as it is to yours.

Do not forget for a moment that the thinking substance is in everything, communicating with everything, and able to influence everything. The desire of the thinking substance for more life and better living has caused the creation of all the sewing machines that have ever been made, and it can cause the creation of millions more. It will do so whenever people set it in motion by desire and faith and by acting in the certain way.

You can certainly have a sewing machine in your house. You can have anything you want, as long as you use it for the advancement of your own life and the lives of others.

You need not hesitate about asking largely. "It is your Father's pleasure to give you the kingdom," said Jesus.

The original substance wants to live as much as possible in you; it wants you to have all that you can or will use for the living of the most abundant life.

Your faith becomes invincible if you fix upon your consciousness the fact that the desire you feel for the possession of riches is one with the desire of the Supreme Power for more complete expression.

Once I saw a little boy sitting at a piano and vainly trying to bring harmony out of the keys. I saw that he was grieved and provoked by his inability to play real music. I asked him why he was unhappy, and he answered, "I can feel the music in me, but I can't make my hands go right." The music in him was the urge of the Original Substance, containing all the possibilities of all life. All that there is of music was seeking expression through the child.

God, the One Substance, is trying to live and do and enjoy things through humanity. He is saying, "I want hands to build wonderful structures, to play divine harmonies, to paint glorious pictures. I want feet to run my errands, eyes to see my beauties, tongues to tell mighty truths and to sing marvelous songs."

All that is possible is seeking expression through human beings. God wants those who can play music to have the instruments they need—to have the means to cultivate their talents to the fullest extent. He wants those who can appreciate beauty to be able to surround themselves with beautiful things. He wants those who can discern truth to have every opportunity to travel and observe. He wants those who can appreciate dress to be beautifully clothed and those who can appreciate good food to be luxuriously fed.

He wants all these things because he enjoys and appreciates them. It is God who wants to play and sing and enjoy beauty and proclaim truth and wear fine clothes and eat good foods.

"It is God that worketh in you to will and to do," said Paul.

The desire you feel for riches is the Infinite, seeking to express himself in you as he sought to find expression in the little boy at the piano.

You need not hesitate to ask largely. Your part is to focus and express the desires of God.

This is a difficult point with most people. They retain something of the old idea that poverty and self—sacrifice are pleasing to God. They look upon poverty as a part of the plan, as a necessity of nature. They have the idea that God has finished his work and has made all that he can make—that the majority of humanity must stay poor because there is not enough to go around. People hold to this erroneous thought so much that they feel ashamed to ask for wealth. They try not to want more than a very modest competence—just enough to make them fairly comfortable.

I recall now the case of one student who was told that he must see in his mind a clear picture of the things he desired so that the creative thought of them might be impressed on the formless substance. He was a very poor man, living in a rented house and having only what he earned from day to day. He could not grasp the fact that all wealth was his. Therefore, after thinking the matter over, he decided that he might reasonably ask for a new rug for the floor of his best room and an anthracite coal stove to heat the house during the cold weather. Following the instructions given in this book, he obtained these things in a few months. Then it dawned upon him that he had not asked enough. He went through the house in which he lived and planned all the improvements he would like to make in it. He mentally added a bay window here and a room there. He continued until it was complete in his mind as his ideal home. And, then he planned its furnishings.

Holding the whole picture in his mind, he began living in the certain way and moving toward what he wanted. He owns the house now, and is rebuilding it according to his mental image. Now, with still larger faith, he is proceeding to get greater things. It has been unto him according to his faith, and it is so with you and with all of us.

CHAPTER 7

Gratitude

The illustrations given in the last chapter will have conveyed to the reader the fact that the first step toward getting rich is to convey the idea of your wants to the formless substance.

This is true, and you will see that in order to do so it becomes necessary to relate yourself to the formless intelligence in a harmonious way.

To secure this harmonious relationship is a matter of such primary and vital importance that I will give some space to its discussion here. I will give you instructions which, if you follow them, will be certain to bring you into a perfect unity of mind with God.

The whole process of mental adjustment and atunement can be summed up in one word—gratitude.

First, you believe that there is one intelligent substance from which all things proceed. Secondly, you believe that this substance gives you everything you desire. And, thirdly, you relate yourself to it through a feeling of deep and profound gratitude.

Many people who order their lives rightly in all other ways are kept in poverty by their lack of gratitude. Having received one gift from God, they cut the wires which connect them with him by failing to make acknowledgment.

It is easy to understand that the nearer we live to the source of wealth, the more wealth we shall receive. It is also easy to understand that a soul that is always grateful lives in closer touch with God than one who never looks to him in thankful acknowledgment.

When good things come to us, the more gratefully we fix our minds on the Supreme Power, the more good things we will receive—and the more rapidly they will come. The reason for this is simply that the mental attitude of gratitude draws the mind into closer touch with the source from which the blessings come.

If it is a new thought to you that gratitude brings your whole mind into closer harmony with the creative energies of the universe, consider it well, and you will see that it is true. The good things you already possess have come to you because of certain laws. Gratitude will lead your mind out along the ways by which things come. And, it will keep you in close harmony with creative thought and prevent you from falling into competitive thought.

Gratitude alone can keep you looking toward the Infinite and prevent you from falling into the error of thinking that the supply of riches is limited—and to think that would be fatal to your hopes.

There is a law of gratitude, and if you are to get the results you seek, it is absolutely necessary that you should observe this law.

The law of gratitude is the natural principle that action and reaction are always equal and in opposite directions. The grateful outreaching of your mind in thankful praise to the Supreme Power is a liberation or expenditure of force; it cannot fail to reach that to which it is addressed. And, as a result, God responds with an instantaneous movement toward you.

"Draw nigh unto God, and He will draw nigh unto you." That is a statement of psychological truth.

And, if your gratitude is strong and constant, the reaction in the formless substance will be strong and continuous. The movement of the things you want will always be toward you. Notice the grateful attitude that Jesus took—how he always seems to be saying, "I thank Thee, Father, that Thou hearest me." You cannot exercise much power without gratitude, because it is gratitude that keeps you connected with power.

But, the value of gratitude does not consist solely in getting more blessings in the future. Without gratitude you cannot keep from being dissatisfied with things as they are.

The moment you permit your mind to dwell with dissatisfaction upon things as they are, you begin to lose ground. You fix attention upon the common, the poor, the squalid, and the mean—and your mind takes the form of these things. You will then transmit these forms or mental images to the formless. Thus, the common, the poor, the squalid, and the mean will come to you.

To permit your mind to dwell upon the inferior is to become inferior and to surround yourself with inferior things. On the other hand, to fix your attention on the best is to surround yourself with the best and to become the best.

The creative power within us makes us into the image of that to which we give our attention. We are thinking substance, and thinking substance always takes the form of that which it thinks about.

The grateful mind is constantly fixed upon the best. Therefore, it tends to become the best; it takes the form or character of the best and will receive the best.

Also, faith is born of gratitude. The grateful mind continually expects good things, and expectation becomes faith. The reaction of gratitude upon one's own mind produces faith. Every outgoing wave of grateful thanksgiving increases faith. The person who has no feeling of gratitude cannot long retain a living faith. And, as we will see in the following chapters, without a living faith you cannot get rich by the creative method.

It is necessary, then, to cultivate the habit of being grateful for every good thing that comes to you—to give thanks continuously. And, because all things have contributed to your advancement, you should include all things in your gratitude.

Do not waste time thinking or talking about the shortcomings or wrong actions of plutocrats or trust magnates. Their organization of the world has made your opportunity. All that you have received really has come to you because of them.

Do not rage against corrupt politicians. If it were not for politicians we should fall into anarchy, and your opportunity would be greatly lessened.

God has worked a long time and very patiently to bring us up to where we are in industry and government. And he is going right on with his work. I believe that he will do away with plutocrats, trust magnates, captains of industry, and politicians as soon as they can be spared. But, in the meantime, they are very necessary. Remember that they are helping to arrange the lines of transmission along which your riches will come to you. Be grateful to them. This will bring you into a harmonious relationship with the good in everything, and the good in everything will move toward you.

CHAPTER 8

Thinking in the Certain Way

Turn back to chapter 6. Read again the story of the man who formed a mental image of his house, and you will get a fair idea of the initial step toward getting rich. You must form a clear and definite mental picture of what you want. You cannot transmit an idea unless you have it yourself.

You must have it before you can give it. And, many people fail to impress the thinking substance because they have themselves only a vague and misty concept of the things they want to do, to have, or to become.

It is not enough that you should have a general desire for wealth "to do good with." Everybody has that desire.

It is not enough that you should have a wish to travel, see things, live more, etc. Everybody has those desires also. If you were going to send a telegram message to a friend, you would not send the letters of the alphabet in their order and let him construct the message for himself. Nor would you take words at random from the dictionary. You would send a coherent sentence; one which meant something. When you try to impress your wishes upon the thinking substance, remember that it must be done by a coherent statement. You must know what you want, and be definite.

You can never get rich or start the creative power into action by sending out unformed longings and vague desires.

Go over your desires just as the man I have described went over his house. See just what you want and get a clear mental picture of it as you wish it to look when you get it.

As the sailor has the port toward which he is sailing in his mind, you must have a clear mental picture continually in your mind. You must keep your face toward it all the time. You must no more lose sight of it than the steerman loses sight of the compass.

It is not necessary to take exercises in concentration, nor to set apart special times for prayer and affirmation, nor to "go into the silence," nor to do occult stunts of any kind. These things are well enough, but all you need is to know what you want and to want it badly enough so that it will stay in your thoughts.

Spend as much of your leisure time as you can in contemplating your picture. Remember that no one needs to take exercises to concentrate his mind on a thing which he really wants. It is the things you do not really care about which require effort to fix your attention upon them.

Unless your desire to get rich is strong enough to hold your thoughts to the purpose—as the magnetic pole holds the needle of the compass—it will hardly be worth while for you to try to carry out the instructions given in this book.

The methods I am presenting here are for people whose desire for riches is strong enough to overcome mental laziness and the love of ease.

The more clear and definite you make your picture, and the more you dwell upon it, the stronger your desire will be. And, the stronger your desire, the easier it will be to hold your mind fixed upon the picture of what you want.

However, something more is necessary than merely seeing the picture clearly. If that is all you do, you are only a dreamer and will have little or no power for accomplishment. Behind your clear vision must be the purpose to realize it, to bring it out in tangible expression. And, behind this purpose must be an invincible and unwavering faith that the thing is already yours—that it is at hand and you have only to take possession of it.

Live in the new house mentally until it takes form around you physically. In the mental realm, enter at once into full enjoyment of the things you want.

"Whatsoever things ye ask for when ye pray, believe that ye receive them, and ye shall have them," said Jesus.

See the things you want as if they were actually around you all the time; see yourself as owning and using them. Make use of them in imagination just as you will use them when they are your tangible possessions. Dwell upon your mental picture until it is clear and distinct. Then, take the mental attitude of ownership toward everything in that picture. Take possession of it in your mind in the full faith that it is actually yours. Hold to this mental ownership; do not waver for an instant in the faith that it is real.

And, remember what was said in chapter 7 about gratitude: be as thankful for it all the time as you expect to be when it has taken form. The person who can sincerely thank God for the things which he owns only in imagination has real faith. That person will get rich; that person will cause the creation of whatsoever he wants.

You do not need to pray repeatedly for the things you want. It is not necessary to tell God about it every day. "Use not vain repetitions as the heathen do," said Jesus to his pupils, "for your Father knoweth that ye have need of these things before ye ask Him."

Your part is to intelligently formulate your desire for the things which make for a larger life and to get these desires arranged into a coherent whole. You must then impress this whole desire upon the formless substance, which has the power and the will to bring you what you want.

You do not make this impression by repeating strings of words: you make it by holding the vision with unshakable purpose to attain it—and with steadfast faith that you will attain it.

The answer to prayer is not according to your faith while you are talking, but according to your faith while you are working.

You cannot impress the mind of God by having a special sabbath day set apart to tell him what you want—and then forgetting him during the rest of the week. If you do not think of your prayer until the hour of prayer comes again, you cannot impress him by having special hours to go into your closet and pray.

Oral prayer has its effect in clarifying your vision and strengthening your faith, but it is not your oral petitions which will get you what you want. In order to get rich you do not need a "sweet hour of prayer." You need to "pray without ceasing." And, by prayer, I mean holding steadily to your vision—with the purpose of causing its creation into solid form and the faith the you are doing so.

"Believe that ye receive them."

Once you have clearly formed your vision, the whole matter turns on receiving. When you have formed it, it is well to make an oral statement by addressing the Supreme Power in reverent prayer. From that moment on you must receive in your mind what you ask for. Live in the new house; wear the fine clothes; ride in the automobile; go on the journey, and confidently plan for greater journeys. Think and speak of all the things you have asked for in terms of actual present ownership. Imagine the exact environment and financial condition you desire and live all the time in that imaginary environment and financial condition. Mind, however, that you do not do this as a mere dreamer and castle builder. Hold to the faith that the imaginary is being realized and to the purpose required to realize it. Remember that it is faith and purpose in the use of the imagination which make the difference between the scientist and the dreamer. And, having learned this fact, it is here the you must learn the proper use of the will.

CHAPTER 9

How to Use the Will

To set about getting rich in a scientific way, you do not try to apply your will power to anything outside of yourself.

You have no right to do so anyway. It is wrong to apply your will to other men and women in order to get them to do what you wish done.

It is as flagrantly wrong to coerce people by mental power as it is to coerce them by physical power. If compelling people by physical force to do things for you reduces them to slavery, compelling them by mental means accomplishes exactly the same thing. The only difference is in the methods. If taking things from people by physical force is robbery, then taking things by mental force is also robbery. In principle there is no difference.

You have no right to use your will power upon another person—even "for his own good"—because you do not know what is for his good.

The science of getting rich does not require you to apply power or force to any other person, in any way whatsoever. There is not the slightest necessity for doing so. Indeed, any attempt to use your will upon others will only tend to defeat your purpose.

You do not need to apply your will to things for them to come to you. That would simply be trying to coerce God and would be foolish and useless, as well as irreverent.

You do not have to compel God to give you good things, any more than you have to use your will power to make the sun rise. You do not have to use your will power to conquer an unfriendly deity or to make stubborn and rebellious forces do your bidding.

The thinking substance is friendly to you and is more anxious to give you what you want than you are to get it.

To get rich, you need only to use your will power upon yourself.

When you know what to think and do, you must use your will to compel yourself to think and do the right things. That is the legitimate use of the will in getting what you want—to use it in holding yourself to the right course. Use your will to keep yourself thinking and acting in the certain way.

Do not try to project your will or your thoughts or your mind out into space to act on things or people. Keep your mind at home. It can accomplish more there than elsewhere.

Use your mind to form a mental image of what you want and to hold that vision with faith and purpose. Use your will to keep your mind working the right way.

The more steady and continuous your faith and purpose, the more rapidly you will get rich, because you will make only positive impressions upon formless substance. You will not neutralize or offset them by negative impressions.

The formless substance receives a picture of your desires and allows this picture to penetrate it to great distances—perhaps, throughout the entire universe.

As this impression spreads, all things are set moving toward its realization. Every living thing, every inanimate things, and the things yet uncreated are stirred toward bringing into being that which you want. All force begins to be exerted in that direction. All things begin to move toward you. The minds of people everywhere are influenced toward doing the things necessary to fulfilling your desires. And, they work for you unconsciously.

But you can check all this by starting a negative impression in the formless substance. Doubt or unbelief is as certain to start a movement away from you as faith and purpose are to start one toward you. By not understanding this, most people fail when they try to make use of "mental science" to get rich. Every hour and moment you spend in giving heed to doubts and fears, every hour you spend in worry, every hour in which your soul is possessed by unbelief—sets a current away from you through the whole domain of the intelligent substance. "All the promises are unto them that believe, and unto them only." Notice how insistent Jesus was upon this point of belief. Now you know the reason why.

Since belief is all important, it behooves you to guard your thoughts. And, as your beliefs will be shaped to a very great extent by the things you observe and think about, it is important that you focus your attention. Here the will comes into use, because by means of your will, you determine the objects of your attention.

If you want to become rich, you must not make a study of poverty. Things are not brought into being by thinking about their opposites. Health is never to be attained by studying disease and thinking about disease. Righteousness is not to be promoted by studying sin and thinking about sin. And, no one ever got rich by studying poverty and thinking about poverty.

Medicine as a science of disease has increased disease. Religion as a science of sin has promoted sin. And, economics as a study of poverty will fill the world with wretchedness and want.

Do not talk about poverty. Do not investigate it or concern yourself with it. Never mind what its causes are. You have nothing to do with them. What concerns you is the cure.

Do not spend your time in charitable work or charity movements. All charity only tends to perpetuate the wretchedness it aims to eradicate.

I do not say that you should be hard—hearted or unkind and refuse to hear the cry of need. But, you must not try to eradicate poverty in any of the conventional ways. Put poverty behind you, put all that pertains to it behind you, and "make good."

You cannot hold the mental image which is necessary to make you rich if you fill your mind with pictures of poverty. Do not read books or papers which give accounts of the wretchedness of the tenement dwellers or of the horrors of child labor. Do not read anything which fills your mind with gloomy images of want and suffering. You cannot help the poor in the least by knowing about these things. The widespread knowledge of the circumstances of the poor does not tend at all to do away with poverty.

What tends to do away with poverty is not the getting of pictures of poverty into your mind, but getting pictures of wealth into the minds of the poor.

You are not deserting the poor in their misery when you refuse to allow your mind to be filled with pictures of that misery.

Poverty can be done away with, not by increasing the number of well-to-do people who think about poverty, but by increasing the number of poor people who succeed in getting rich through the exercise of faith and purpose.

The poor do not need charity. They need inspiration. Charity only sends them a loaf of bread to keep them alive in their wretchedness or gives them an entertainment to make them forget for an hour or two. But, inspiration will cause them to rise out of their misery. If you want to help the poor, demonstrate to them that they can become rich; prove it by getting rich yourself. Get rich. This is the best way that you can help the poor.

The only way in which poverty will ever be banished from this world is by getting a large and constantly increasing number of people to practice the teachings of this book.

People must be taught to become rich by creation, not by competition.

Every person who becomes rich by competition kicks down the ladder by which he rises and keeps others down. But, every person who gets rich by creation opens a way for thousands to follow him and inspires them to do so.

You are not showing hardness of heart or an unfeeling disposition when you refuse to pity poverty or to think or talk about it or to listen to those who do talk about it. Use your will power to keep your mind off the subject of poverty and to keep your mind fixed with faith and purpose on the vision of what you want.

CHAPTER 10

Further Use of the Will

You cannot retain a true and clear vision of wealth if you are constantly turning your attention to opposing pictures, either external or imaginary.

Do not tell others of any past financial troubles. Do not think of them at all. Do not tell anyone about the poverty of your parents or the hardships of your early life. To do any of these things is to mentally class yourself with the poor for the time being, and this will certainly check the movement of things in your direction.

"Let the dead bury their dead," as Jesus said.

Put poverty and all things that pertain to poverty completely behind you.

You have accepted a certain theory of the universe as being correct and are resting all your hopes of happiness on its being correct. What can you gain by giving heed to conflicting theories?

Do not read religious books which tell you that the world is soon coming to an end. Do not read the writings of muckrakers and pessimistic philosophers who tell you that it is going to the devil. The world is not going to the devil. It is going to God. It is a wonderful becoming.

True, there may be a good many things in existing conditions which are disagreeable. But, what is the use of studying them when they are certainly passing away and when the study of them only tends to check their passing and keep them with us? Why give time and attention to things which are being removed by evolutionary growth, when you can hasten their removal only by promoting the evolutionary growth as far as your part of it goes?

No matter how horrible the apparent conditions may be in certain countries, sections, or places, you waste your time and destroy your own chances by considering them. You should interest yourself in the world's becoming rich.

Think of the riches the world is coming into, instead of the poverty it is growing out of. And, bear in mind that the only way in which you can assist the world in growing rich is by growing rich yourself through the creative method—not the competitive one.

Give your attention wholly to riches; ignore poverty. Whenever you think or speak of those who are poor, think and speak of them as those who are becoming rich—as those who are to be congratulated rather than pitied. Then they and others will catch the inspiration and begin to search for the way out.

Because I say that you are to give your whole time and mind and thought to riches, it does not follow that you are to be sordid or mean.

To become really rich is the noblest aim you can have in life because it includes everything else.

On the competitive plane, the struggle to get rich is a godless scramble for power over other people, but when we come into the creative mind, all this is changed.

All that is possible in the way of greatness and soul unfoldment—of service and lofty endeavor—comes by way of getting rich. All is made possible by the use of things.

If you do not have physical health, you will find that its attainment is conditional on your getting rich. Only those who are emancipated from financial worry and who have the means to live a carefree existence and follow hygienic practices can have and retain health.

Moral and spiritual greatness is only possible for those who are above the competitive battle for existence. And, only those who are becoming rich on the plane of creative thought are free from the degrading influences of competition. If your heart is set on domestic happiness, remember that love flourishes best where there is refinement, a high level of thought, and freedom from corrupting influences. These are to be found only where riches are attained without strife or rivalry by the exercise of creative thought.

I repeat: you can aim at nothing so great or noble as to become rich. You must fix your attention upon your mental picture of riches—to the exclusion of all that may tend to dim or obscure your vision.

You must learn to see the underlying truth in all things. You must see beneath all seemingly wrong conditions the great one life ever moving forward toward fuller expression and more complete happiness.

It is the truth that there is no such thing as poverty. There is only wealth.

Some people remain in poverty because they are ignorant of the fact that there is wealth for them. These people can best be taught by showing them the way to affluence in your own person and practice.

Others are poor because, while they feel that there is a way out, they are too intellectually indolent to put forth the mental effort necessary to find that way and travel it. And, for these people, the very best thing you can do is to arouse their desire by showing them the happiness that comes from being rightly rich.

Others are poor because, while they have some notion of science, they have become so swamped and lost in a maze of metaphysical and occult theories that they do not know which road to take. They try a mixture of many systems and fail in all. For these, again, the very best thing to do is to show them the right way in your own person and practice. An ounce of doing things is worth a pound of theorizing.

The very best thing you can do for the whole world is to make the most of yourself.

You can serve God and your fellow humans in no more effective way than by getting rich. That is, if you get rich by the creative method and not by the competitive one.

Another thing. I assert that this book gives in detail the principies of the science of getting rich. You do not need to read any other book upon the subject. This may sound narrow and egotistical. However, there is no more scientific method of computation in mathematics than by addition, subtraction, multiplication, and division. No other method is possible. There can be only one shortest distance between two points.

There is only one way to think scientifically, and that is to think in the way that leads by the most direct and simple route to the goal. No person has yet formulated a briefer or less complex system than the one I am describing here. It has been stripped of all nonessentials. When you begin this method, lay all others aside. Put them out of your mind altogether.

Read this book every day. Keep it with you. Commit it to memory. Do not think about other systems and theories. If you do, you will begin to have doubts and to become uncertain and wavering in your thought. Then you will bring negative thought to the formless substance.

After you have made good and become rich, you may study other systems as much as you please. But, until you are quite sure that you have gained what you want, do not read anything else on this subject except the authors mentioned in the preface.

Only read the most optimistic comments on the world's news, just those that are in harmony with your picture.

Also, postpone your investigations into the occult. Do not dabble in theosophy, spiritualism, or kindred studies. It is very likely that the dead still live and are near. But, if they are, let them alone. Mind your own business.

Wherever the spirits of the dead may be, they have their own work to do and their own problems to solve. We have no right to interfere with them. We cannot help them. It is very doubtful whether they can help us or whether we have any right to trespass upon their time if they can. Let the dead and the hereafter alone. Solve your own problem; get rich. If you begin to mix with the occult, you will start mental crosscurrents which will surely bring your hopes to shipwreck. Lastly, this and the preceding chapters have brought us to the following statement of basic facts:

> *There is a thinking stuff from which all things are made, and which, in its original state, permeates, penetrates, and fills the interspaces of the universe.*
>
> *A thought in this substance produces the thing that is imagined by the thought.*

A person can form things in his thought, and by impressing his thought upon formless substance, can cause the thing he thinks about to be created.

In order to do this, a person must pass from the competitive to the creative mind. He must form a clear mental picture of the things he wants. And, he must hold this picture in his thoughts with the fixed purpose to get what he wants and the unwavering faith that he will get what he wants—closing his mind against all that may tend to shake his purpose, dim his vision, or quench his faith.

And, in addition to all this, we shall now see that he must live and act in the certain way.

CHAPTER 11

Acting in the Certain Way

Thought is the impelling force which causes the creative power to act. Thinking in the certain way will bring riches to you, but you must not rely upon thought alone, paying no attention to personal action. That is the rock upon which many otherwise scientific metaphysical thinkers meet shipwreck—the failure to connect thought with personal action.

We have not yet reached the stage of development, in which a person can create directly from the formless substance without nature's processes or the work of human hands. A person must act as well as think.

By thought you can cause the gold in the hearts of the mountains to be impelled toward you. But, it will not mine itself, refine itself, coin itself into double eagles, and come rolling along the roads into your pocket.

Under the impelling force of the Supreme Power, people's affairs will be so ordered that someone will be led to mine the gold for you. And, another person's business transactions will be so directed that the gold will be brought toward you. You must arrange your own business affairs so that you are able to receive it when it comes to you. Your thought makes all things, animate and inanimate, work to bring you what you want. However, your personal activity must be such that you can rightly receive what you want when it reaches you. You are not to take it as charity or steal it. You must give every person more in use value than he gives you in cash value.

The scientific use of thought consists in forming a clear and distinct mental image of what you want, in holding fast to your purpose to get what you want, and in realizing with grateful faith that you do get what you want.

Do not try to project your thought in any mysterious or occult way with the idea of having it go out and do things for you. That is wasted effort and will weaken your power to think with sanity.

In the preceding chapters, I have fully explained the action of thought in getting rich. You must use your faith and purpose to positively impress your vision upon the formless substance, which has the same desire for more life that you have. And, this vision, received from you, sets all the creative forces at work in and through their regular channels of action, but directed toward you.

It is not your part to guide or supervise the creative process. All you have to do with that is to retain your vision, stick to your purpose, and maintain your faith and gratitude.

But you must act in the certain way so that you can appropriate what is yours when it comes to you—so that you can accept the things in your picture and put them in their proper places.

You can readily see the truth of this. When things reach you, they will be in the hands of other people who will ask an equivalent for them.

You can only get what is yours by giving the other person what is his.

Your pocketbook will not become bottomless; it will not always be full of money without effort on your part.

Receiving is the crucial point in the science of getting rich—right here, where thought and personal action must be combined. There are many people who, consciously or unconsciously, set the creative forces in action by the strength and persistence of their desires. However, they remain poor because they do not provide for the reception of the thing they want when it comes.

By thought, the thing you want is brought to you. By action, you receive it.

Whatever your action is to be, it is evident that you must act now. You cannot act in the past. It is essential to the clearness of your mental vision that you dismiss the past from your mind. You cannot act in the future because the future is not here yet. And, you cannot tell how you will want to act in any future contingency until that contingency has arrived.

Because you are not in the right business or the right environment now, do not think that you must postpone action until you get into the right business or environment. And, do not spend time in the present planning the best course in possible future emergencies. Have faith in your ability to meet any emergency when it arrives.

If you act in the present with your mind on the future, your present action will be with a divided mind and will not be effective. Put your whole mind into present action.

Do not give your creative impulse to the original substance and then sit down and wait for results; if you do, you will never get them. Act now. There is never any time but now, and there never will be any time but now. If you are ever to begin to make ready for the reception of what you want, you must begin now.

Your action must be in your present business or employment and must be upon the persons and things in your present environment.

You cannot act where you are not. You cannot act where you have been, and you cannot act where you are going to be. You can act only where you are.

Do not dwell on whether yesterday's work was well or poorly done. Do today's work well.

Do not try to do tomorrow's work now. There will be plenty of time to do that when tomorrow comes.

Do not try by occult or mystical means to act on people or things that are out of your reach.

Do not wait for a change of environment before you act. Cause a change of environment through action.

You can act upon your present environment so as to cause yourself to be transferred to a better environment.

Hold with faith and purpose the vision of yourself in the better environment, but act upon your present environment with all your heart and with all your strength and with all your mind.

Do not spend any time in day dreaming or castle building. Hold to the one vision of what you want, and act now.

Do not cast about seeking some new thing to do or some strange, unusual, or remarkable action to perform as a first step toward getting rich. For some time to come your actions will probably be the same as those you have been performing. But, now you will perform those actions in the certain way which will surely make you rich.

If you are engaged in some business and feel that it is not the right one for you, do not wait until you get into the right business before you begin to act. Do not feel discouraged or sit down and lament because you are in the wrong place. No person was ever so misplaced that he could not find the right place, and no person was ever so involved in the wrong business that he could not get into the right business.

Hold the vision of yourself in the right business with the purpose to get into it and the faith that you will get into it. But, act in your present business. Use your present business as the means of getting a better one, and use your present environment as the means of getting into a better one. Your vision of the right business, if held with faith and purpose, will cause the Supreme Power to move the right business toward you. And, your action—if performed in the certain way—will cause you to move toward the business.

If you are an employee and feel that you must change places in order to get what you want, do not project your thought into space and rely upon it to get you another job. It will probably fail to do so. Hold the vision of yourself in the job you want, while you act with faith and purpose on the job you have, and you will certainly get the job you want.

Your vision and faith will set the creative force in motion to bring it toward you. And, your action will cause the forces in your own environment to move you toward the place you want. In closing this chapter, I will add another statement to our syllabus:

> *There is a thinking stuff from which all things are made, and which, in its original state, permeates, penetrates, and fills the interspaces of the universe.*
>
> *A thought in this substance produces the thing that is imaged by the thought.*

A person can form things in his thought, and by impressing his thoughts upon formless substance, can cause the thing he thinks about to be created.

In order to do this, a person must pass from the competitive to the creative mind. He must form a clear mental picture of the things he wants. And, he must hold this picture in his thoughts with the fixed purpose to get what he wants, and the unwavering faith that he will get what he wants—closing his mind to all that may tend to shake his purpose, dim his vision, or quench his faith.

That he may receive what he wants when it comes, a person must act now upon the people and things in his present environment.

CHAPTER 12

Efficient Action

You must use your thought as I have directed in the previous chapters. You must begin to do what you can do where you are, and you must do all that you can do where you are.

You can advance only by being larger than your present place. And, no man is larger than his present place who leaves undone any of the work pertaining to that place.

The world is advanced only by those who more than fill their present places.

If no one quite filled his present place, there would be a backslide in everything. Those who do not quite fill their present places are a dead weight upon society, government, commerce, and industry. They must be carried along by others at a great expense. The progress of the world is retarded only by those who do not fill the places they are holding. They belong to a former age and a lower stage or plane of life. Their tendency is toward degeneration. No society could advance if every individual was smaller than his place because social evolution is guided by the law of physical and mental evolution. In the animal world, evolution is caused by an excess of life.

When an organism has more life than can be expressed in the functions of its own plane, it develops the organs of a higher plane, and a new species is originated.

There never would have been new species had there not been organisms which more than filled their places. The law is exactly the same for you. Your getting rich depends upon your applying this principle to your own affairs.

Every day is either a successful day or a day of failure. And, it is the successful days which get you what you want. If every day is a failure, you can never get rich; if every day is a success, you cannot help but get rich.

If there is something that may be done today and you do not do it, you have failed in so far as that thing is concerned. And, the consequences may be more disastrous than you imagine.

You cannot foresee the results of even the most trivial act. You do not know the workings of all the forces that have been set moving in your behalf. Much may be depending on your doing some simple act; it may be the very thing which is to open the door of opportunity to great possibilities. You can never know all the combinations which Supreme Power is making for you in the world of things and of human affairs. Your neglect or failure to do some small thing may cause a long delay in getting you what you want.

Do, every day, all that can be done that day.

There is, however, a limitation or qualification that you must take into account. You are not to overwork or to rush blindly into your business in the effort to do the greatest possible number of things in the shortest possible time.

You are not to try to do tomorrow's work today or to do a week's work in a day.

It is really not the number of things you do, but the efficiency of each separate action that counts.

Every act is, in itself, either efficient or inefficient. Every inefficient act is a failure, and if you spend your life doing inefficient acts, your whole life will be a failure. The more things you do, the worse for you, if all your acts are inefficient ones.

On the other hand, every efficient act is a success in itself, and if every act of your life is an efficient one, your whole life must be a success.

The cause of failure is doing too many things in an inefficient manner and not doing enough things in an efficient manner.

You will see that it is a self-evident proposition that if you do not do any inefficient acts and if you do a sufficient number of efficient acts, you will become rich. If it is possible for you to make each act an efficient one, you see again that the getting of riches is reduced to an exact science, like mathematics.

The matter turns, then, on the question of whether you can make each separate act a success in itself. And, this you can certainly do.

You can make each act a success, because the Infinite is working with you, and the Infinite cannot fail.

The Supreme Power is at your service. To make each act efficient you have only to put your own power into it.

Every action is either strong or weak. When everyone is strong, you are acting in the certain way which will make you rich.

Every act can be made strong and efficient by holding your vision while you are doing it and by putting the whole power of your faith and purpose into it.

It is at this point that the people who separate mental power from personal action fail. They use the power of mind in one place and at one time, and they act in another place and at another time. Thus, their acts are not successful in themselves; too many of them are inefficient. But, if you put the Supreme Power in every act, no matter how commonplace, every act will be a success in itself. Every success opens the way to other successes. Your progress toward what you want, and the movement of what you want toward you will become increasingly rapid.

Remember that successful action is cumulative in its results. When a man begins to move toward a larger life, more things attach themselves to him, and the influence of his desire is multiplied. This is because the desire for life is inherent in all things.

Do, every day, all that you can do that day, and do each act in an efficient manner.

In saying that you must hold your vision while you are doing each act—however trivial or common place! do not mean to say that it is necessary at all times to see the vision distinctly to its smallest details. During your leisure hours, you should focus your imagination on the details of your vision in order to fix it firmly in your memory.

If you wish speedy results, spend practically all your spare time in this practice. By continuous contemplation you will get the picture of what you want firmly fixed upon your mind and completely transferred to the mind of the formless substance. Then, in your working hours, you need only to mentally refer to the picture to stimulate your faith and purpose and to put forth your best effort. Contemplate your picture in your leisure hours until your consciousness is so full of it that you can grasp it instantly. You will become so enthusiastic about its bright promises that the mere thought of it will call forth the strongest energies of your whole being.

Let us again repeat our syllabus, and by slightly changing the closing statements, bring it to the point we have now reached.

> *There is a thinking stuff from which all things are made, and which, in its original state, permeates, penetrates, and fills the interspaces of the universe.*
>
> *A thought in this substance produces the thing that is imagined by the thought.*
>
> *A person can form things in his though t, and by impressing his thought upon form less substance, can cause the thing he thinks about to be created.*
>
> *In order to do this, a person must pass from the competitive to the creative mind. He must form a clear mental picture of the things he wants. And, he must do with faith and purpose all that can be done each day—doing each separate thing in an efficient manner.*

CHAPTER 13

Getting into the Right Business

Success, in any particular business, depends for one thing upon your possessing in a well-developed state the faculties required in that business.

Without good musical faculty no one can succeed as a teacher of music. Without exceptional mechanical abilities no one can achieve great success in any of the mechanical trades. Without tact and a flair for commerce no one can succeed in the mercantile pursuits. But, to possess in a well-developed state the faculties required in your particular vocation does not ensure getting rich. There are musicians who have remarkable talent, and who yet remain poor. There are blacksmiths and carpenters who have excellent mechanical ability, but who do not get rich. And, there are merchants with good skills for dealing with people who nevertheless fail.

The different faculties are tools. It is essential to have good tools, but it is also essential that the tools should be used in the right way. One man can take a sharp saw, a square, and a good plane and build a handsome article of furniture. Another man can take the same tools and set to work to duplicate the article, but his production will be a botch. He does not know how to use good tools in a successful way.

The various faculties of your mind are the tools with which you must do the work which is to make you rich. It will be easier for you to succeed if you get into a business for which you are well-equipped with mental tools.

Generally speaking, you will do best in that business which will use your strongest faculties—the one for which you are naturally "best fitted." But there are also limitations to this statement. No one should regard his vocation as being irrevocably fixed by the skills with which he was born.

You can get rich in any business because if you have not the right talent for it, you can develop that talent. It merely means that you will have to make your tools as you go along, instead of confining yourself to the use of those with which you were born. It will be easier for you to succeed in a vocation for which you already have the talents in a well-developed state. But, you can succeed in any vocation because you can develop any rudimentary talent, and there is no talent of which you have not at least a small amount.

You will get rich most easily if you do that for which you are best fitted. But, you will get rich most satisfactorily if you do that which you want to do.

Doing what you want to do is life. And, there is no real satisfaction in living if we are compelled to do something which we do not like to do and fail to do what we want to do. And, it is certain that you can do what you want to do; your desire to do it is proof that you have within you the power which can do it.

Desire is a manifestation of power.

The desire to play music is a power seeking expression and development. The desire to invent mechanical devices is also a power seeking expression and development.

Where there is no power—either developed or undeveloped—to do a thing, there is never any desire to do that thing. Where there is a strong desire to do a thing, it is proof that the power to do it is strong and only needs to be developed and applied in the right way.

All things being equal, it is best to select a business for which you have the best developed talent. But, if you have a strong desire to engage in any particular line of work, you should select that work as the ultimate goal.

Because you can do what you want to do, it is your right and privilege to follow the business or avocation which will be most congenial and pleasant.

You are not obliged to do what you do not like to do and should not do it except as a means to bring you to your desired work.

If there are past mistakes whose consequences have placed you in an undesirable business or environment, you may be obliged for some time to do what you do not like to do. But, you can make the doing of it pleasant by knowing that it is making it possible for you to come to your desired work.

If you feel that you are not in the right vocation, do not act too hastily in trying to get into another one. The best way, generally, to change a business or an environment is by growth.

Do not be afraid to make a sudden and radical change if the opportunity is presented and if you feel after careful consideration that it is the right opportunity. But, never take sudden or radical action when you are in doubt as to the wisdom of doing so.

There is never any hurry on the creative plane. And there is no lack of opportunity.

When you get out of the competitive mind, you will understand that you never need to act hastily. No one else is going to beat you to the thing you want to do. There is enough for all. If one place is taken, another and a better one will be opened for you a little farther on. There is plenty of time. When you are in doubt, wait. Fall back on the contemplation of your vision and increase your faith and purpose. And, by all means, in times of doubt and indecision, cultivate gratitude.

A day or two spent in contemplating the vision of what you want and in earnest thanksgiving that you are getting it will bring your mind into such close relationship with the Infinite that you will make no mistake when you do act.

There is a mind which knows all there is to know. And, if you have deep gratitude, you can come into close unity with this mind by faith and the purpose to advance in life.

Mistakes come from acting hastily or from acting in fear or doubt or in forgetfulness of the right motive—which is more life to all and less to none.

As you go on in the certain way, opportunities will come to you in increasing numbers. You will need to be very steady in your faith and purpose and to keep in close touch with the Supreme Power through reverent gratitude.

Do all that you can do in a perfect manner every day, but do it without haste, worry, or fear. Go as fast as you can, but never hurry.

Remember that in the moment you begin to hurry you cease to be a creator and become a competitor. You drop back into the old plane again.

Whenever you find yourself hurrying, stop. Fix your attention on the mental image of the thing you want and begin to give thanks that you are getting it. This exercise of gratitude will never fail to strengthen your faith and renew your purpose.

CHAPTER 14

The Impression of Increase

Whether you change your vocation or not, you must direct your present actions to the business in which you are presently engaged.

You can get into the business you want by making constructive use of the business you are already established in—by doing your daily work in the certain way.

And, in so far as your business consists in dealing with other people—whether directly, by telephone, or by letter—the key thought of all your efforts must be to convey to their minds the impression of increase.

Increase is what all men and all women are seeking. It is the urge of the formless intelligence within them to find fuller expression.

The desire for increase is inherent in all nature. It is the fundamental impulse of the universe. All human activities are based on the desire for increase. People are seeking more food, more clothes, better shelter, more luxury, more beauty, more knowledge, more pleasure—more life.

Every living thing is under that necessity for continuous advancement. Where increase of life ceases, dissolution and death set in at once.

People instinctively know this, and hence they are forever seeking more. This law of perpetual increase is set forth by Jesus in the parable of the talents. Only those who gain more retain any. "From him who hath not shall be taken away even that which he hath."

The normal desire for increased wealth is not an evil or a reprehensible thing. It is simply the desire for more abundant life. And, because it is the deepest instinct of their natures, all men and women are attracted to an individual who can give them more of the means of life.

In following the certain way—as described in the foregoing pages—you are getting continuous increase for yourself, and you are giving it to all with whom you deal. You are a creative center from which increase is given off to all.

Be sure of this, and convey assurance of this fact to every man, woman, and child with whom you come in contact. No matter how small the transaction—even if it is only selling of a stick of candy to a little child—put into this action the thought of increase and make sure that the customer is impressed with the thought.

Convey the impression of advancement with everything you do, so that all people shall receive the impression that you are an advancing man and that you advance all who deal with you. Also, give people who you meet socially the thought of increase.

You can convey this impression by holding the unshakable faith that you are in the way of increase and by letting this faith inspire, fill, and permeate every action. Do everything that you do in the firm conviction that you are an advancing personality, and that you are giving advancement to everybody. Feel that you are getting rich, and that in so doing you are making others rich—that you are conferring benefits on all.

Do not boast or brag of your success or talk about it unnecessarily. True faith is never boastful.

Wherever you find a boastful person, you find one who is secretly doubtful and afraid. Simply feel the faith and let it work out in every transaction. Let every act and tone and look express the quiet assurance that you are getting rich—that you are already rich. Words will not be necessary to communicate this feeling to others. They will feel the sense of increase when they are in your presence, and will be attracted to you.

You must so impress others that they will feel that in associating with you they will get increase for themselves. See that you give them a use value greater than the cash value you are taking from them.

If you always take an honest pride in doing this and let everybody know it, you will always have customers. People will go where they are given increase; and the Supreme Power—which desires increase in everything and which knows everything—will move toward you men and women who have never heard of you. Your business will increase rapidly, and you will be surprised at the unexpected benefits which will come to you. You will be able to make larger combinations, to secure greater advantages, and to go on into a more congenial vocation if you desire to do so.

However, in doing all this, you must never lose sight of your vision of what you want or of your faith and purpose.

Let me here give you another word of caution in regard to motives: beware of the insidious temptation to seek power over other people.

Nothing is so pleasant to the unformed or partially developed mind as the exercise of power or domination over others. The desire to rule for selfish gratification has been the curse of the world. For countless ages, kings and lords have drenched the earth with blood in their battles to extend their dominions. They have not been engaged in an effort to seek more life for all, but to get more power for themselves.

Today, the main motive in the business and industrial world is the same. People marshal their armies of dollars and lay waste the lives and hearts of millions in the same mad scramble for power over others. Commercial kings, like political kings, are inspired by the lust for power.

Jesus saw in this desire for mastery the moving impulse of that evil world he sought to overthrow. Read 23 Matthew and see how he pictures the lust of the Pharisees to be called "master," to sit in the high places, to domineer over others, and to lay burdens on the backs of the less fortunate. Note how he compares this lust for dominion to the brotherly seeking for the common good to which he calls his disciples.

Look out for the temptation to seek authority, to become a master, to be considered as one who is above the common herd, and to impress others by lavish display.

The mind that seeks for mastery over others is the competitive mind, and the competitive mind is not the creative one. In order to master your environment and your destiny, it is not at all necessary that you should rule over your fellows. And, indeed, when you fall into the world's struggle for high places, you begin to be conquered by fate and environment and getting rich becomes a matter of chance and speculation.

Beware of the competitive mind! No better statement of the principle of creative action can be formulated than the favorite declaration of the late Golden Rule Jones: "What I want for myself, I want for everybody."

CHAPTER 15

The Advancing Man

What I have said in the last chapter applies to the professional and the wage earner as well as to a person who is engaged in mercantile business.

No matter what your profession, if you can give increase of life to others and make them sensible of this gift, they will be attracted to you, and you will get rich. The physician who holds the vision of himself as a great and successful healer—and who works toward the complete realization of that vision with faith and purpose—will come into such close touch with the Infinite that he will be phenomenally successful. Patients will come to him in throngs.

No one has a greater opportunity to carry into effect the teachings of this book than the practitioner of medicine. It does not matter which of the various schools he may belong to, because the principle of healing is common to all of them and may be reached by all. The advancing man in medicine—who holds to a clear mental image of himself as successful and who obeys the laws of faith, purpose, and gratitude—will cure every curable case he undertakes, no matter what remedies he may use.

In the field of religion, the world cries out for clergy who can teach their hearers the true science of abundant life. A person who masters the details of the science of getting rich—together with the allied sciences of being well, of being great, and of winning love—and who teaches these details from the pulpit, will never lack for a congregation. This is the gospel that the world needs. It will give increase of life. People will hear it gladly and will give liberal support to the person who brings it to them.

What is now needed is a demonstration of the science of life from the pulpit. We want preachers who can not only tell us how, but who in their own persons will show us how. We need the preacher who is rich, healthy, great, and beloved, to teach us how to attain these things. And, when that person comes, he will find a numerous and loyal following.

The same is true of the teacher who can inspire the children with the faith and purpose of the advancing life. That person will never be out of a job. And teachers who have this faith and purpose can give it to their pupils. They cannot help giving it to them if it is part of their own life and practice.

What is true of the teacher, preacher, and physician is also true of the lawyer, dentist, real estate person, insurance agent—of everybody.

The combined mental and personal action I have described is infallible. It cannot fail. Every man and woman who follows these instructions steadily, perseveringly, and to the letter will get rich. The law of the increase of life is as mathematically certain in its operation as the law of gravitation. Getting rich is an exact science.

The wage earner will also find this to be true. Do not feel that you have no chance to get rich because you are working where there is no visible opportunity for advancement—where wages are small and the cost of living high. Form your clear mental vision of what you want and begin to act with faith and purpose.

Do all the work you can do, every day, and do each piece of work in a perfectly successful manner. Put the power of success and the purpose of getting rich into everything that you do. However, do not do this merely with the idea of currying favor with your employer in the hope that he, or those above you, will see your good work and advance you. It is unlikely that they will do so.

The person who is merely a good worker—filling his place to the very best of his ability and satisfied with that—is valuable to his employer. It is not in the employer's interest to promote him. He is worth more where he is.

To secure advancement, something more is necessary than to be too large for your place. The person who is certain to advance is the one who is too big for his place and who has a clear concept of what he wants to be—who knows that he can become what he wants to be and who is determined to be what he wants to be.

Do not try to more than fill your present place with a view to pleasing your employer. Do it with the idea of advancing yourself. Hold the faith and purpose of increase during work hours, after work hours, and before work hours. Hold it in such a way that every person who comes in contact with you—whether foreman, fellow worker, or social acquaintance—will feel the power of purpose radiating from you. Hold the faith and purpose so that everyone will get the sense of advancement and increase from you. People will be attracted to you, and if there is no possibility for advancement in your present job, you will very soon see an opportunity to take another job.

There is a power which never fails to present opportunity to the advancing man who is moving in obedience to law.

God cannot help helping you if you act in the certain way. He must do so in order to help himself.

There is nothing in your circumstances or in the industrial situation that can keep you down. If you cannot get rich working for a conglomerate, you can get rich on a ten-acre farm. And, if you begin to move in the certain way, you will certainly escape from the clutches of the conglomerates and get on to the farm or wherever else you wish to be.

If a few thousand of its employees would enter upon the certain way, a company would soon be in a bad plight. It would have to give its workers more opportunity or go out of business. Nobody has to work for inadequate pay. The company can keep people in so-called hopeless conditions only so long as there are those who are too ignorant to know of the science of getting rich—or too intellectually slothful to practice it.

Begin this way of thinking and acting, and your faith and purpose will allow you to quickly see any opportunity to better your condition.

Such opportunities will speedily come because the Supreme Power, working in everything and working for you, will bring opportunities to you.

Do not wait for an opportunity to be all that you want to be. When an opportunity to be more than you are now is presented and you feel impelled toward it, take it. It will be the first step toward a still greater opportunity.

There is no such thing possible in this universe as a lack of opportunities for a person who is living the advancing life.

It is inherent in the constitution of the cosmos that all things shall be for the advancing man and work together for his good. And, he must certainly get rich if he acts and thinks in the certain way. So let wage earning men and women study this book with great care and enter with confidence upon the course of action I prescribe. It will not fail.

CHAPTER 16

Cautions and Concluding Observations

Many people will scoff at the idea that there is an exact science of getting rich. Holding the impression that the supply of wealth is limited, they will insist that social and governmental institutions must be changed before a considerable number of people can acquire wealth.

But, this is not true.

It is true that existing governments keep the masses in poverty, but this is because the masses do not think and act in a certain way. If the masses began to move forward according to my suggestions, neither governments nor industrial systems could check them. All systems would have to be modified to accommodate this forward movement.

If the people had the advancing mind and had the faith that they can become rich, nothing could possibly keep them in poverty.

Individuals may enter upon the certain way—at any time and under any government—and make themselves rich. And, when a considerable number of individuals do so under any government, they will cause the system to be modified so as to open the way for others.

The more men who get rich on the competitive plane, the worse for others. The more who get rich on the creative plane, the better for others.

The economic salvation of the masses can only be accomplished by encouraging a large number of people to become rich by practicing the scientific method set down in this book. These people will show others the way and inspire them with a desire for real life—with the faith that it can be attained and with the purpose to attain it.

For the present, however, it is enough to know that neither the government under which you live nor the capitalistic or competitive system of industry can keep you from getting rich. When you enter upon the creative plane of thought, you will rise above all these things and become a citizen of another kingdom.

But, remember that your thought must stay on the creative plane. You are never to regard the supply as limited or to act in a competitive manner.

Whenever you do fall into old ways of thought, correct yourself instantly, because when you are in the competitive mind, you have lost the cooperation of the Supreme Power.

Do not spend any time in planning how you will meet possible emergencies in the future. You should be concerned with doing today's work in a perfectly successful manner—not with emergencies which may arise tomorrow. You can attend to them as they come.

Do not concern yourself with questions of how you will surmount obstacles which may loom upon your business horizon. Ignore these questions unless you can plainly see that your course must be altered today in order to avoid these obstacles.

No matter how tremendous an obstruction may appear at a distance, you will find that if you continue in the certain way, it will disappear as you approach it—or that a way over, through, or around it will appear.

No possible combination of circumstances can defeat a man or woman who is proceeding to get rich along strictly scientific lines. No man or woman who obeys the law can fail to get rich—any more than one can multiply two by two and fail to get four.

Give no anxious thought to possible disasters, obstacles, panics, or unfavorable combinations of circumstances. There is time enough to meet such things when they present themselves before you in the immediate present You will find that every difficulty carries with it the wherewithal for its overcoming.

Guard your speech. Never speak of yourself, your affairs, or of anything else in a discouraged or discouraging way.

Never admit the possibility of failure or speak in a way that implies failure as a possibility.

Never speak of the times as being hard or of business conditions as being doubtful. Times may be hard and business doubtful for those who are on the competitive plane, but they can never be so for you. You can create what you want, and you are above fear.

When others are having hard times and poor business, you will find your greatest opportunities.

Train yourself to think of and to look upon the world as a something which is becoming—which is growing—and to regard seeming evil as being only that which is undeveloped. Always speak in terms of advancement. To do otherwise is to deny your faith, and to deny your faith is to lose it.

Never allow yourself to feel disappointed. You may expect to have a certain thing at a certain time and not get it at that time. This will seem to be a failure. But, if you hold to your faith, you will find that the failure is only apparent.

Go on in the certain way, and if you do not receive that thing, you will receive something so much better that you will see that the seeming failure was a prelude to a great success.

A student of the science of getting rich had set his mind on making a certain business combination which at the time seemed to him to be very desirable. He worked for some weeks to bring it about. When the crucial time came, the thing failed in a perfectly inexplicable way. It was as if some unseen influence had been working secretly against him. He was not disappointed. On the contrary, he thanked God that his desire had been overruled and went steadily on with a grateful mind. In a few weeks, an opportunity so much better came his way that now he would not have made the first deal on any account. He saw that a mind which knew more than he knew had prevented him from losing the greater good by entangling himself with the lesser.

That is the way every seeming failure will work out for you—if you keep your faith, hold to your purpose, have gratitude, and each day, do all that can be done that day.

When you make a failure, it is because you have not asked enough. Keep on, and a larger thing than you were seeking will certainly come to you. Remember this.

You will not fail because you lack the necessary talent to do what you wish to do. If you go on as I have directed, you will develop all the talent that is necessary for doing your work.

It is not within the scope of this book to deal with the science of cultivating talent. But, it is as certain and simple as the process of getting rich.

However, do not hesitate or waver for fear that when you come to a place where you will fail for lack of ability. Keep right on, and when you come to that place, the ability will be furnished to you. The same source of ability, which enabled the untaught Lincoln to do the greatest work in government ever accomplished by a single man, is open to you. You may draw upon the thinking mind to use in meeting the responsibilities which are laid upon you. Proceed in full faith.

Study this book. Make it your constant companion until you have mastered all the ideas contained in it. While you are getting firmly established in this faith, you will do well to give up most recreations and pleasures and to stay away from places where conflicting ideas are advanced in lectures or sermons. Do not read pessimistic or conflicting literature. Do very little reading outside of the writers mentioned in the introduction. Spend most of your leisure time in contemplating your vision, in cultivating gratitude, and in reading this book. It contains all you need to know of the science of getting rich. And, you will find all the essentials summed up in the following chapter.

CHAPTER 17

A Summary of the Science of Getting Rich

There is a thinking stuff from which all things are made, and which, in its original state, permeates, penetrates, and fills the interspaces of the universe.

A thought in this substance produces the thing that is imagined by the thought.

A person can form things in his thought, and by impressing his thought upon formless substance, can cause the thing he thinks about to be created.

In order to do this, a person must pass from the competitive to the creative mind. Otherwise, he cannot be in harmony with the formless intelligence, which is always creative and never competitive in spirit.

A person can come into full harmony with the formless substance by entertaining a lively and sincere sense of gratitude for the blessings it bestows upon him. Gratitude unifies a person's mind with the thinking mind so that an individual's thoughts are received by the formless substance. A person can remain on the creative plane only by uniting himself with the formless intelligence through a deep and continuous feeling of gratitude.

An individual must form a clear and definite mental image of the things he wishes to have, do, or become. And, he must hold this mental image in his thoughts while being deeply grateful to the Supreme Power for granting him all of his desires. The person who wishes to get rich must spend his leisure hours in contemplating his vision and in earnest thanksgiving that this reality is being given to him. Too much stress cannot be laid on the importance of frequent contemplation of the mental image—coupled with unwavering faith and devout gratitude. This is the process by which the impression is given to the formless substance and the creative forces set in motion.

The creative energy works through the established channels of natural growth and through present industrial and social order. All that is included in his mental image will surely be brought to the person who follows my instructions and whose faith does not waver. What he wants will come to him through the ways of established trade and commerce.

A person must be active in order to receive his own when it is ready to come to him. He must more than fill his present place. He must keep in mind the purpose is to get rich through realization of his mental image. He must do every day all that can be done that day—taking care to do each act in a successful manner. He must give to every man a use value in excess of the cash value he receives—so that each transaction makes for more life. And, he must hold the advancing thought so that the impression of increase will be communicated to all with whom he comes in contact.

The men and women who practice the foregoing instructions will certainly get rich. And, the riches they receive will be in exact proportion to the definiteness of their vision, the fixity of their purpose, the steadiness of their faith, and the depth of their gratitude.

Can You Answer these Questions on the Science of Getting Rich?

These questions constitute a thorough examination on this book and a complete outline of the science of financial success. Write out the answer to each question with thoughtful consideration. As far as possible, do so without consulting the book—making sure that you have the principles and practices of the science thoroughly fixed in your memory. Then, reread the chapters and correct your answers. This practice will help you immeasurably in the recognition, realization, and application of this book's principles.

CHAPTER 1

1. Show that the right to life includes the right to be rich. Tell why in full.
2. Is it right to be content with honest poverty? If not, why not? How rich do you want to be?
3. Explain what a complete life is and show how riches are essential to complete living.
4. In which department of your life—body, mind, or soul—do you feel the greatest lack?

CHAPTER 2

1. What causes the ownership of money and property?
2. Prove that getting rich is not a matter of environment.
3. Prove that getting rich is not the result of superior talent.

4. Prove that getting rich is not the result of saving or thrift.
5. Prove that getting rich is not the result of doing things that are neglected or overlooked by others.
6. Prove that doing things in a certain way is not too difficult to follow.
7. Show how much location is important in getting rich.

CHAPTER 3

1. Show that opportunity cannot be monopolized.
2. Prove that the world's workers have their future in their own hands.
3. What is meant by the "invisible supply"?

CHAPTER 4

1. How does thought create from the formless substance?
2. What is man, and what power has he?
3. Repeat the summary from page 22. Do you understand it? Do you believe it? How can it be proved?
4. What is the basic fact behind all appearances?
5. What must you do and what must you believe if you are to practice the science of getting rich?

CHAPTER 5

1. Prove that God wants you to get rich, and tell why.
2. Why is it essential that your purpose should harmonize with the purpose of the Supreme Power? What is the purpose of the Supreme Power?
3. Why can you help others more by making the most of yourself than in any other way?
4. What is the difference between creation and competition?
5. Explain why God has made plutocrats and monopolists.
6. Why don't riches gained on the competitive plane cause happiness?
7. How are you to keep from falling into the competitive mind?

CHAPTER 6

1. Explain the difference between use value and market value, and show how one can make a profit without robbing another.
2. If you have wage earners in your employ, what can you do to atone for the unfairness of the wage system?
3. Can you cause things to be formed directly from the atmosphere by thought? How can you cause creation? Explain the process.
4. Is it a mistake to ask for a modest competence when you can use more?

CHAPTER 7

1. What are the three steps by which you enter into relationship with the Supreme Power?
2. Explain why and how gratitude keeps you in close touch with God.
3. Explain the operation of the law of action and reaction.
4. Read the four gospels with a special view to studying the attitude of Jesus towards the Father and say what you think of it. How does it compare with the attitude suggested by this book?
5. Why should you fix your mind on the best?
6. Explain the relation between gratitude and faith.
7. Explain why and how all things are good.

CHAPTER 8

1. What is the most important thing to do to make an impression on the thinking substance?
2. What is the difference between the dreamer and the person who uses the imagination scientifically?
3. Give your idea as to what constitutes a scientific use of the imagination.
4. Are you working with faith and purpose?

CHAPTER 9

1. Tell in your own language why you have no right to apply your willpower to other people.
2. Can you compel the things you want to come to you by exerting willpower? If not, why not?
3. Can you keep your mind thinking as you want it to think? If not, what hinders you?
4. Tell how positive and negative impressions are made on the formless substance.
5. What should be your attitude toward poverty?

CHAPTER 10

1. What about telling others about your past troubles?
2. Explain the use of the will in properly directing the attention.

CHAPTER 11

1. Why is it impossible to get rich by thought without personal action?
2. What must you do if you are in the wrong business or location?
3. How should an employee proceed to get a better job?

CHAPTER 12

1. How much should you try to do each day? Why?
2. What is the cause of evolution?
3. How can you make each act efficient?
4. Do you feel that you are acting efficiently now? If not, why not?
5. What is said in this chapter about the vision?

CHAPTER 13

1. If you have a pronounced talent for some particular business, what should you do?
2. In what way are faculties like tools?

3. What is desire? How does the desire to do a thing prove that you can do the thing?
4. What should you do when tempted to act hastily?

CHAPTER 14

1. Why do all people desire increase?
2. What assurance should you seek to convey to others?
3. What temptation is spoken of? How much power do you want? Why do you want power?

CHAPTER 15

1. What impression should the professional person seek to give? Why?
2. What should a worker do who is where there is no visible chance for advancement?
3. What would happen to a company if a few thousand of its employees entered the certain way?

CHAPTER 16

1. Show why existing governments do not keep the people in poverty.
2. What will accomplish the economic salvation of the masses?
3. What about planning for future emergencies and obstacles?
4. Give the scientific reason for refusing to worry.
5. What are you to do if what you want does not come when you expect it? Give the reason.
6. What about tasks which look too great for your ability?

CHAPTER 17

1. Give, in your own words, a summary of the science of getting rich.

THE ART OF MONEY GETTING

or

Golden Rules for Making Money

P. T. Barnum

Introduction

In the United States, where we have more land than people, it is not at all difficult for persons in good health to make money. In this comparatively new field there are so many avenues of success open, so many vocations which are not crowded, that any person of either sex who is willing, at least for the time being, to engage in any respectable occupation that offers, may find lucrative employment.

Those who really desire to attain an independence, have only to set their minds upon it, and adopt the proper means, as they do in regard to any other object which they wish to accomplish, and the thing is easily done. But however easy it may be found to make money, I have no doubt many of my hearers will agree it is the most difficult thing in the world to keep it. The road to wealth is, as Dr. Franklin truly says, "as plain as the road to the mill." It consists simply in expending less than we earn; that seems to be a very simple problem. Mr. Micawber, one of those happy creations of the genial Dickens, puts the case in a strong light when he says that to have annual income of twenty pounds per annum, and spend twenty pounds and sixpence, is to be the most miserable of men; whereas, to have an income of only twenty pounds, and spend but nineteen pounds and sixpence is to be the happiest of mortals. Many of my readers may say, "we understand this: this is economy, and we know economy is wealth; we know we can't eat our cake and keep it also." Yet I beg to say that perhaps more cases of failure arise from mistakes on this point than almost any other. The fact is, many people think they understand economy when they really do not.

True economy is misapprehended, and people go through life without properly comprehending what that principle is. One says, "I have an income of so much, and here is my neighbor who has the same; yet every year he gets something ahead and I fall short; why is it? I know all about economy." He thinks he does, but he does not. There are men who think that economy consists in saving cheese-parings and candle-ends, in cutting off two pence from the laundress' bill and doing all sorts of little, mean, dirty things. Economy is not meanness. The misfortune is, also, that this class of persons let their economy apply in only one direction. They fancy they are so wonderfully economical in saving a half-penny where they ought to spend twopence, that they think they can afford to squander in other directions. A few years ago, before kerosene oil was discovered or thought of, one might stop overnight at almost any farmer's house in the agricultural districts and get a very good supper, but after supper he might attempt to read in the sitting-room, and would find it impossible with the inefficient light of one candle. The hostess, seeing his dilemma, would say: "It is rather difficult to read here evenings; the proverb says 'you must have a ship at sea in order to be able to burn two candles at once;' we never have an extra candle except on extra occasions." These extra occasions occur, perhaps, twice a year. In this way the good woman saves five, six, or ten dollars in that time: but the information which might be derived from having the extra light would, of course, far outweigh a ton of candles.

But the trouble does not end here. Feeling that she is so economical in tallow candies, she thinks she can afford to go frequently to the village and spend twenty or thirty dollars for ribbons and furbelows, many of which are not necessary. This false connote may frequently be seen in men of business, and in those instances it often runs to writing-paper. You find good businessmen who save all the old envelopes and scraps, and would not tear a new sheet of paper, if they could avoid it, for the world. This is all very well; they may in this way save five or ten dollars a year, but being so economical (only in note paper), they think they can afford to waste time; to have expensive parties, and to drive their carriages. This is an illustration of Dr. Franklin's "saving at the spigot and wasting at the bung-hole;" "penny wise and pound foolish." Punch in speaking of this "one idea" class of people says "they are like the man who bought a penny herring for his family's dinner and then hired a coach and four to take it home." I never knew a man to succeed by practising this kind of economy.

True economy consists in always making the income exceed the out-go. Wear the old clothes a little longer if necessary; dispense with the new pair of gloves; mend the old dress: live on plainer food if need be; so that, under all circumstances, unless some unforeseen accident occurs, there will be a margin in favor of the income. A penny here, and a dollar there, placed at interest, goes on accumulating, and in this way the desired result is attained. It requires some training, perhaps, to accomplish this economy, but when once used to it, you will find there is more satisfaction in rational saving than in irrational spending. Here is a recipe which I recommend: I have found it to work an excellent cure for extravagance, and especially for mistaken economy: When you find that you have no surplus at the end of the year, and yet have a good income, I advise you to take a few sheets of paper and form them into a book and mark down every item of expenditure. Post it every day or week in two columns, one headed "necessaries" or even "comforts", and the other headed "luxuries," and you will find that the latter column will be double, treble, and frequently ten times greater than the former. The real comforts of life cost but a small portion of what most of us can earn. Dr. Franklin says "it is the eyes of others and not our own eyes which ruin us. If all the world were blind except myself I should not care for fine clothes or furniture." It is the fear of what Mrs. Grundy may say that keeps the noses of many worthy families to the grindstone. In America many persons like to repeat "we are all free and equal," but it is a great mistake in more senses than one.

That we are born "free and equal" is a glorious truth in one sense, yet we are not all born equally rich, and we never shall be. One may say; "there is a man who has an income of fifty thousand dollars per annum, while I have but one thousand dollars; I knew that fellow when he was poor like myself; now he is rich and thinks he is better than I am; I will show him that I am as good as he is; I will go and buy a horse and buggy; no, I cannot do that, but I will go and hire one and ride this afternoon on the same road that he does, and thus prove to him that I am as good as he is."

My friend, you need not take that trouble; you can easily prove that you are "as good as he is;" you have only to behave as well as he does; but you cannot make anybody believe that you are rich as he is. Besides, if you put on these "airs," add waste your time and spend your money, your poor wife will be obliged to scrub her fingers off at home, and buy her tea two ounces at a time, and everything else in proportion, in order that you may keep up "appearances," and, after all, deceive nobody. On the other hand, Mrs. Smith may say that her next-door neighbor married Johnson for his money, and "everybody says so." She has a nice one-thousand dollar camel's hair shawl, and she will make Smith get her an imitation one, and she will sit in a pew right next to her neighbor in church, in order to prove that she is her equal.

My good woman, you will not get ahead in the world, if your vanity and envy thus take the lead. In this country, where we believe the majority ought to rule, we ignore that principle in regard to fashion, and let a handful of people, calling themselves the aristocracy, run up a false standard of perfection, and in endeavoring to rise to that standard, we constantly keep ourselves poor; all the time digging away for the sake of outside appearances. How much wiser to be a "law unto ourselves" and say, "we will regulate our out-go by our income, and lay up something for a rainy day." People ought to be as sensible on the subject of money-getting as on any other subject. Like causes produces like effects. You cannot accumulate a fortune by taking the road that leads to poverty. It needs no prophet to tell us that those who live fully up to their means, without any thought of a reverse in this life, can never attain a pecuniary independence.

Men and women accustomed to gratify every whim and caprice, will find it hard, at first, to cut down their various unnecessary expenses, and will feel it a great self-denial to live in a smaller house than they have been accustomed to, with less expensive furniture, less company, less costly clothing, fewer servants, a less number of balls, parties, theater-goings, carriage-ridings, pleasure excursions, cigar-smokings, liquor-drinkings, and other extravagances; but, after all, if they will try the plan of laying by a "nest-egg," or, in other words, a small sum of money, at interest or judiciously invested in land, they will be surprised at the pleasure to be derived from constantly adding to their little "pile," as well as from all the economical habits which are engendered by this course.

The old suit of clothes, and the old bonnet and dress, will answer for another season; the Croton or spring water taste better than champagne; a cold bath and a brisk walk will prove more exhilarating than a ride in the finest coach; a social chat, an evening's reading in the family circle, or an hour's play of "hunt the slipper" and "blind man's buff" will be far more pleasant than a fifty or five hundred dollar party, when the reflection on the difference in cost is indulged in by those who begin to know the pleasures of saving. Thousands of men are kept poor, and tens of thousands are made so after they have acquired quite sufficient to support them well through life, in consequence of laying their plans of living on too broad a platform. Some families expend twenty thousand dollars per annum, and some much more, and would scarcely know how to live on less, while others secure more solid enjoyment frequently on a twentieth part of that amount. Prosperity is a more severe ordeal than adversity, especially sudden prosperity. "Easy come, easy go," is an old and true proverb. A spirit of pride and vanity, when permitted to have full sway, is the undying canker-worm which gnaws the very vitals of a man's worldly possessions, let them be small or great, hundreds, or millions. Many persons, as they begin to prosper, immediately expand their ideas and commence expending for luxuries, until in a short time their expenses swallow up their income, and they become ruined in their ridiculous attempts to keep up appearances, and make a "sensation."

I know a gentleman of fortune who says, that when he first began to prosper, his wife would have a new and elegant sofa. "That sofa," he says, "cost me thirty thousand dollars!" When the sofa reached the house, it was found necessary to get chairs to match; then side-boards, carpets and tables "to correspond" with them, and so on through the entire stock of furniture; when at last it was found that the house itself was quite too small and old-fashioned for the furniture, and a new one was built to correspond with the new purchases; "thus," added my friend, "summing up an outlay of thirty thousand dollars, caused by that single sofa, and saddling on me, in the shape of servants, equipage, and the necessary expenses attendant upon keeping up a fine 'establishment,' a yearly outlay of eleven thousand dollars, and a tight pinch at that: whereas, ten years ago, we lived with much more real comfort, because with much less care, on as many hundreds. The truth is," he continued, "that sofa would have brought me to inevitable bankruptcy, had not a most unexampled title to prosperity kept me above it, and had I not checked the natural desire to 'cut a dash.'"

The foundation of success in life is good health: that is the substratum fortune; it is also the basis of happiness. A person cannot accumulate a fortune very well when he is sick. He has no ambition; no incentive; no force. Of course, there are those who have bad health and cannot help it: you cannot expect that such persons can accumulate wealth, but there are a great many in poor health who need not be so.

If, then, sound health is the foundation of success and happiness in life, how important it is that we should study the laws of health, which is but another expression for the laws of nature! The nearer we keep to the laws of nature, the nearer we are to good health, and yet how many persons there are who pay no attention to natural laws, but absolutely transgress them, even against their own natural inclination. We ought to know that the "sin of ignorance" is never winked at in regard to the violation of nature's laws; their infraction always brings the penalty. A child may thrust its finger into the flames without knowing it will burn, and so suffers, repentance, even, will not stop the smart. Many of our ancestors knew very little about the principle of ventilation. They did not know much about oxygen, whatever other "gin" they might have been acquainted with; and consequently they built their houses with little seven-by-nine feet bedrooms, and these good old pious Puritans would lock themselves up in one of these cells, say their prayers and go to bed. In the morning they would devoutly return thanks for the "preservation of their lives," during the night, and nobody had better reason to be thankful. Probably some big crack in the window, or in the door, let in a little fresh air, and thus saved them.

Many persons knowingly violate the laws of nature against their better impulses, for the sake of fashion. For instance, there is one thing that nothing living except a vile worm ever naturally loved, and that is tobacco; yet how many persons there are who deliberately train an unnatural appetite, and overcome this implanted aversion for tobacco, to such a degree that they get to love it. They have got hold of a poisonous, filthy weed, or rather that takes a firm hold of them. Here are married men who run about spitting tobacco juice on the carpet and floors, and sometimes even upon their wives besides. They do not kick their wives out of doors like drunken men, but their wives, I have no doubt, often wish they were outside of the house. Another perilous feature is that this artificial appetite, like jealousy, "grows by what it feeds on;" when you love that which is unnatural, a stronger appetite is created for the hurtful thing than the natural desire for what is harmless. There is an old proverb which says that "habit is second nature," but an artificial habit is stronger than nature. Take for instance, an old tobacco-chewer; his love for the "quid" is stronger than his love for any particular kind of food. He can give up roast beef easier than give up the weed.

Young lads regret that they are not men; they would like to go to bed boys and wake up men; and to accomplish this they copy the bad habits of their seniors. Little Tommy and Johnny see their fathers or uncles smoke a pipe, and they say, "If I could only do that, I would be a man too; uncle John has gone out and left his pipe of tobacco, let us try it." They take a match and light it, and then puff away. "We will learn to smoke; do you like it Johnny?" That lad dolefully replies: "Not very much; it tastes bitter;" by and by he grows pale, but he persists and he soon offers up a sacrifice on the altar of fashion; but the boys stick to it and persevere until at last they conquer their natural appetites and become the victims of acquired tastes.

I speak "by the book," for I have noticed its effects on myself, having gone so far as to smoke ten or fifteen cigars a day; although I have not used the weed during the last fourteen years, and never shall again. The more a man smokes, the more he craves smoking; the last cigar smoked simply excites the desire for another, and so on incessantly.

Take the tobacco-chewer. In the morning, when he gets up, he puts a quid in his mouth and keeps it there all day, never taking it out except to exchange it for a fresh one, or when he is going to eat; oh! yes, at intervals during the day and evening, many a chewer takes out the quid and holds it in his hand long enough to take a drink, and then pop it goes back again. This simply proves that the appetite for rum is even stronger than that for tobacco. When the tobacco-chewer goes to your country seat and you show him your grapery and fruit house, and the beauties of your garden, when you offer him some fresh, ripe fruit, and say, "My friend, I have got here the most delicious apples, and pears, and peaches, and apricots; I have imported them from Spain, France and Italy—just see those luscious grapes; there is nothing more delicious nor more healthy than ripe fruit, so help yourself; I want to see you delight yourself with these things;" he will roll the dear quid under his tongue and answer, "No, I thank you, I have got tobacco in my mouth." His palate has become narcotized by the noxious weed, and he has lost, in a great measure, the delicate and enviable taste for fruits. This shows what expensive, useless and injurious habits men will get into. I speak from experience. I have smoked until I trembled like an aspen leaf, the blood rushed to my head, and I had a palpitation of the heart which I thought was heart disease, till I was almost killed with fright. When I consulted my physician, he said "break off tobacco using." I was not only injuring my health and spending a great deal of money, but I was setting a bad example. I obeyed his counsel. No young man in the world ever looked so beautiful, as he thought he did, behind a fifteen cent cigar or a meerschaum!

These remarks apply with tenfold force to the use of intoxicating drinks. To make money, requires a clear brain. A man has got to see that two and two make four; he must lay all his plans with reflection and forethought, and closely examine all the details and the ins and outs of business. As no man can succeed in business unless he has a brain to enable him to lay his plans, and reason to guide him in their execution, so, no matter how bountifully a man may be blessed with intelligence, if the brain is muddled, and his judgment warped by intoxicating drinks, it is impossible for him to carry on business successfully. How many good opportunities have passed, never to return, while a man was sipping a "social glass," with his friend! How many foolish bargains have been made under the influence of the "nervine," which temporarily makes its victim think he is rich. How many important chances have been put off until to-morrow, and then forever, because the wine cup has thrown the system into a state of lassitude, neutralizing the energies so essential to success in business. Verily, "wine is a mocker." The use of intoxicating drinks as a beverage, is as much an infatuation, as is the smoking of opium by the Chinese, and the former is quite as destructive to the success of the business man as the latter. It is an unmitigated evil, utterly indefensible in the light of philosophy; religion or good sense. It is the parent of nearly every other evil in our country.

Don't Mistake Your Vocation

The safest plan, and the one most sure of success for the young man starting in life, is to select the vocation which is most congenial to his tastes. Parents and guardians are often quite too negligent in regard to this. It very common for a father to say, for example: "I have five boys. I will make Billy a clergyman; John a lawyer; Tom a doctor, and Dick a farmer." He then goes into town and looks about to see what he will do with Sammy. He returns home and says "Sammy, I see watchmaking is a nice genteel business; I think I will make you a goldsmith." He does this, regardless of Sam's natural inclinations, or genius.

We are all, no doubt, born for a wise purpose. There is as much diversity in our brains as in our countenances. Some are born natural mechanics, while some have great aversion to machinery. Let a dozen boys of ten years get together, and you will soon observe two or three are "whittling" out some ingenious device; working with locks or complicated machinery. When they were but five years old, their father could find no toy to please them like a puzzle. They are natural mechanics; but the other eight or nine boys have different aptitudes. I belong to the latter class; I never had the slightest love for mechanism; on the contrary, I have a sort of abhorrence for complicated machinery. I never had ingenuity enough to whittle a cider tap so it would not leak. I never could make a pen that I could write with, or understand the principle of a steam engine. If a man was to take such a boy as I was, and attempt to make a watchmaker of him, the boy might, after an apprenticeship of five or seven years, be able to take apart and put together a watch; but all through life he would be working up hill and seizing every excuse for leaving his work and idling away his time. Watchmaking is repulsive to him.

Unless a man enters upon the vocation intended for him by nature, and best suited to his peculiar genius, he cannot succeed. I am glad to believe that the majority of persons do find their right vocation. Yet we see many who have mistaken their calling, from the blacksmith up (or down) to the clergyman. You will see, for instance, that extraordinary linguist the "learned blacksmith," who ought to have been a teacher of languages; and you may have seen lawyers, doctors and clergymen who were better fitted by nature for the anvil or the lapstone.

Select the Right Location

After securing the right vocation, you must be careful to select the proper location. You may have been cut out for a hotel keeper, and they say it requires a genius to "know how to keep a hotel." You might conduct a hotel like clock-work, and provide satisfactorily for five hundred guests every day; yet, if you should locate your house in a small village where there is no railroad communication or public travel, the location would be your ruin. It is equally important that you do not commence business where there are already enough to meet all demands in the same occupation. I remember a case which illustrates this subject. When I was in London in 1858, I was passing down Holborn with an English friend and came to the "penny shows." They had immense cartoons outside, portraying the wonderful curiosities to be seen "all for a penny." Being a little in the "show line" myself, I said "let us go in here." We soon found ourselves in the presence of the illustrious showman, and he proved to be the sharpest man in that line I had ever met. He told us some extraordinary stories in reference to his bearded ladies, his Albinos, and his Armadillos, which we could hardly believe, but thought it "better to believe it than look after the proof." He finally begged to call our attention to some wax statuary, and showed us a lot of the dirtiest and filthiest wax figures imaginable. They looked as if they had not seen water since the Deluge.

"What is there so wonderful about your statuary?" I asked.

"I beg you not to speak so satirically," he replied, "Sir, these are not Madam Tussaud's wax figures, all covered with gilt and tinsel and imitation diamonds, and copied from engravings and photographs.

Mine, sir, were taken from life. Whenever you look upon one of those figures, you may consider that you are looking upon the living individual."

Glancing casually at them, I saw one labeled "Henry VIII," and feeling a little curious upon seeing that it looked like Calvin Edson, the living skeleton, I said: "Do you call that 'Henry the Eighth?'" He replied, "Certainly; sir; it was taken from life at Hampton Court, by special order of his majesty; on such a day."

He would have given the hour of the day if I had resisted; I said, "Everybody knows that 'Henry VIII.' was a great stout old king, and that figure is lean and lank; what do you say to that?"

"Why," he replied, "you would be lean and lank yourself if you sat there as long as he has."

There was no resisting such arguments. I said to my English friend, "Let us go out; do not tell him who I am; I show the white feather; he beats me."

He followed us to the door, and seeing the rabble in the street, he called out, "ladies and gentlemen, I beg to draw your attention to the respectable character of my visitors," pointing to us as we walked away. I called upon him a couple of days afterwards; told him who I was, and said:

"My friend, you are an excellent showman, but you have selected a bad location."

He replied, "This is true, sir; I feel that all my talents are thrown away; but what can I do?"

"You can go to America," I replied. "You can give full play to your faculties over there; you will find plenty of elbowroom in America; I will engage you for two years; after that you will be able to go on your own account."

He accepted my offer and remained two years in my New York Museum. He then went to New Orleans and carried on a traveling show business during the summer. To-day he is worth sixty thousand dollars, simply because he selected the right vocation and also secured the proper location. The old proverb says, "Three removes are as bad as a fire," but when a man is in the fire, it matters but little how soon or how often he removes.

Avoid Debt

Young men starting in life should avoid running into debt. There is scarcely anything that drags a person down like debt. It is a slavish position to get in, yet we find many a young man, hardly out of his "teens," running in debt. He meets a chum and says, "Look at this: I have got trusted for a new suit of clothes." He seems to look upon the clothes as so much given to him; well, it frequently is so, but, if he succeeds in paying and then gets trusted again, he is adopting a habit which will keep him in poverty through life. Debt robs a man of his self-respect, and makes him almost despise himself. Grunting and groaning and working for what he has eaten up or worn out, and now when he is called upon to pay up, he has nothing to show for his money; this is properly termed "working for a dead horse." I do not speak of merchants buying and selling on credit, or of those who buy on credit in order to turn the purchase to a profit. The old Quaker said to his farmer son, "John, never get trusted; but if thee gets trusted for anything, let it be for 'manure,' because that will help thee pay it back again."

Mr. Beecher advised young men to get in debt if they could to a small amount in the purchase of land, in the country districts. "If a young man," he says, "will only get in debt for some land and then get married, these two things will keep him straight, or nothing will." This may be safe to a limited extent, but getting in debt for what you eat and drink and wear is to be avoided. Some families have a foolish habit of getting credit at "the stores," and thus frequently purchase many things which might have been dispensed with.

It is all very well to say; "I have got trusted for sixty days, and if I don't have the money the creditor will think nothing about it." There is no class of people in the world, who have such good memories as creditors. When the sixty days run out, you will have to pay. If you do not pay, you will break your promise, and probably resort to a falsehood. You may make some excuse or get in debt elsewhere to pay it, but that only involves you the deeper.

A good-looking, lazy young fellow, was the apprentice boy, Horatio. His employer said, "Horatio, did you ever see a snail?" "I—think—I—have," he drawled out. "You must have met him then, for I am sure you never overtook one," said the "boss." Your creditor will meet you or overtake you and say, "Now, my young friend, you agreed to pay me; you have not done it, you must give me your note." You give the note on interest and it commences working against you; "it is a dead horse." The creditor goes to bed at night and wakes up in the morning better off than when he retired to bed, because his interest has increased during the night, but you grow poorer while you are sleeping, for the interest is accumulating against you.

Money is in some respects like fire; it is a very excellent servant but a terrible master. When you have it mastering you; when interest is constantly piling up against you, it will keep you down in the worst kind of slavery. But let money work for you, and you have the most devoted servant in the world. It is no "eye-servant." There is nothing animate or inanimate that will work so faithfully as money when placed at interest, well secured. It works night and day, and in wet or dry weather.

I was born in the blue-law State of Connecticut, where the old Puritans had laws so rigid that it was said, "they fined a man for kissing his wife on Sunday." Yet these rich old Puritans would have thousands of dollars at interest, and on Saturday night would be worth a certain amount; on Sunday they would go to church and perform all the duties of a Christian. On waking up on Monday morning, they would find themselves considerably richer than the Saturday night previous, simply because their money placed at interest had worked faithfully for them all day Sunday, according to law!

Do not let it work against you; if you do there is no chance for success in life so far as money is concerned. John Randolph, the eccentric Virginian, once exclaimed in Congress, "Mr. Speaker, I have discovered the philosopher's stone: pay as you go." This is, indeed, nearer to the philosopher's stone than any alchemist has ever yet arrived.

Persevere

When a man is in the right path, he must persevere. I speak of this because there are some persons who are "born tired;" naturally lazy and possessing no self-reliance and no perseverance. But they can cultivate these qualities, as Davy Crockett said:

"This thing remember, when I am dead: Be sure you are right, then go ahead."

It is this go-aheaditiveness, this determination not to let the "horrors" or the "blues" take possession of you, so as to make you relax your energies in the struggle for independence, which you must cultivate.

How many have almost reached the goal of their ambition, but, losing faith in themselves, have relaxed their energies, and the golden prize has been lost forever.

It is, no doubt, often true, as Shakespeare says:

"There is a tide in the affairs of men, Which, taken at the flood, leads on to fortune."

If you hesitate, some bolder hand will stretch out before you and get the prize. Remember the proverb of Solomon: "He becometh poor that dealeth with a slack hand; but the hand of the diligent maketh rich."

Perseverance is sometimes but another word for self-reliance. Many persons naturally look on the dark side of life, and borrow trouble. They are born so. Then they ask for advice, and they will be governed by one wind and blown by another, and cannot rely upon themselves. Until you can get so that you can rely upon yourself, you need not expect to succeed.

I have known men, personally, who have met with pecuniary reverses, and absolutely committed suicide, because they thought they could never overcome their misfortune. But I have known others who have met more serious financial difficulties, and have bridged them over by simple perseverance, aided by a firm belief that they were doing justly, and that Providence would "overcome evil with good." You will see this illustrated in any sphere of life.

Take two generals; both understand military tactics, both educated at West Point, if you please, both equally gifted; yet one, having this principle of perseverance, and the other lacking it, the former will succeed in his profession, while the latter will fail. One may hear the cry, "the enemy are coming, and they have got cannon."

"Got cannon?" says the hesitating general.

"Yes."

"Then halt every man."

He wants time to reflect; his hesitation is his ruin; the enemy passes unmolested, or overwhelms him; while on the other hand, the general of pluck, perseverance and self-reliance, goes into battle with a will, and, amid the clash of arms, the booming of cannon, the shrieks of the wounded, and the moans of the dying, you will see this man persevering, going on, cutting and slashing his way through with unwavering determination, inspiring his soldiers to deeds of fortitude, valor, and triumph.

Whatever You Do, Do It with All Your Might

Work at it, if necessary, early and late, in season and out of season, not leaving a stone unturned, and never deferring for a single hour that which can be done just as well now. The old proverb is full of truth and meaning, "Whatever is worth doing at all, is worth doing well." Many a man acquires a fortune by doing his business thoroughly, while his neighbor remains poor for life, because he only half does it. Ambition, energy, industry, perseverance, are indispensable requisites for success in business.

Fortune always favors the brave, and never helps a man who does not help himself. It won't do to spend your time like Mr. Micawber, in waiting for something to "turn up." To such men one of two things usually "turns up:" the poorhouse or the jail; for idleness breeds bad habits, and clothes a man in rags. The poor spendthrift vagabond says to a rich man:

"I have discovered there is enough money in the world for all of us, if it was equally divided; this must be done, and we shall all be happy together."

"But," was the response, "if everybody was like you, it would be spent in two months, and what would you do then?"

"Oh! divide again; keep dividing, of course!"

I was recently reading in a London paper an account of a like philosophic pauper who was kicked out of a cheap boarding-house because he could not pay his bill, but he had a roll of papers sticking out of his coat pocket, which, upon examination, proved to be his plan for paying off the national debt of England without the aid of a penny. People have got to do as Cromwell said: "not only trust in Providence, but keep the powder dry." Do your part of the work, or you cannot succeed. Mahomet, one night, while encamping in the desert, overheard one of his fatigued followers remark: "I will loose my camel, and trust it to God!" "No, no, not so," said the prophet, "tie thy camel, and trust it to God!" Do all you can for yourselves, and then trust to Providence, or luck, or whatever you please to call it, for the rest.

DEPEND UPON YOUR OWN PERSONAL EXERTIONS.

The eye of the employer is often worth more than the hands of a dozen employees. In the nature of things, an agent cannot be so faithful to his employer as to himself. Many who are employers will call to mind instances where the best employees have overlooked important points which could not have escaped their own observation as a proprietor. No man has a right to expect to succeed in life unless he understands his business, and nobody can understand his business thoroughly unless he learns it by personal application and experience. A man may be a manufacturer: he has got to learn the many details of his business personally; he will learn something every day, and he will find he will make mistakes nearly every day. And these very mistakes are helps to him in the way of experiences if he but heeds them. He will be like the Yankee tin-peddler, who, having been cheated as to quality in the purchase of his merchandise, said: "All right, there's a little information to be gained every day; I will never be cheated in that way again." Thus a man buys his experience, and it is the best kind if not purchased at too dear a rate.

I hold that every man should, like Cuvier, the French naturalist, thoroughly know his business. So proficient was he in the study of natural history, that you might bring to him the bone, or even a section of a bone of an animal which he had never seen described, and, reasoning from analogy, he would be able to draw a picture of the object from which the bone had been taken. On one occasion his students attempted to deceive him. They rolled one of their number in a cow skin and put him under the professor's table as a new specimen. When the philosopher came into the room, some of the students asked him what animal it was. Suddenly the animal said "I am the devil and

I am going to eat you." It was but natural that Cuvier should desire to classify this creature, and examining it intently, he said:

"Divided hoof; graminivorous! It cannot be done."

He knew that an animal with a split hoof must live upon grass and grain, or other kind of vegetation, and would not be inclined to eat flesh, dead or alive, so he considered himself perfectly safe. The possession of a perfect knowledge of your business is an absolute necessity in order to insure success.

Among the maxims of the elder Rothschild was one, all apparent paradox: "Be cautious and bold." This seems to be a contradiction in terms, but it is not, and there is great wisdom in the maxim. It is, in fact, a condensed statement of what I have already said. It is to say; "you must exercise your caution in laying your plans, but be bold in carrying them out." A man who is all caution, will never dare to take hold and be successful; and a man who is all boldness, is merely reckless, and must eventually fail. A man may go on "'change" and make fifty, or one hundred thousand dollars in speculating in stocks, at a single operation. But if he has simple boldness without caution, it is mere chance, and what he gains to-day he will lose to-morrow. You must have both the caution and the boldness, to insure success.

The Rothschilds have another maxim: "Never have anything to do with an unlucky man or place." That is to say, never have anything to do with a man or place which never succeeds, because, although a man may appear to be honest and intelligent, yet if he tries this or that thing and always fails, it is on account of some fault or infirmity that you may not be able to discover but nevertheless which must exist.

There is no such thing in the world as luck. There never was a man who could go out in the morning and find a purse full of gold in the street to-day, and another to-morrow, and so on, day after day: He may do so once in his life; but so far as mere luck is concerned, he is as liable to lose it as to find it. "Like causes produce like effects." If a man adopts the proper methods to be successful, "luck" will not prevent him. If he does not succeed, there are reasons for it, although, perhaps, he may not be able to see them.

Use the Best Tools

Men in engaging employees should be careful to get the best. Understand, you cannot have too good tools to work with, and there is no tool you should be so particular about as living tools. If you get a good one, it is better to keep him, than keep changing. He learns something every day; and you are benefited by the experience he acquires. He is worth more to you this year than last, and he is the last man to part with, provided his habits are good, and he continues faithful. If, as he gets more valuable, he demands an exorbitant increase of salary; on the supposition that you can't do without him, let him go. Whenever I have such an employee, I always discharge him; first, to convince him that his place may be supplied, and second, because he is good for nothing if he thinks he is invaluable and cannot be spared.

But I would keep him, if possible, in order to profit from the result of his experience. An important element in an employee is the brain. You can see bills up, "Hands Wanted," but "hands" are not worth a great deal without "heads." Mr. Beecher illustrates this, in this wise:

An employee offers his services by saying, "I have a pair of hands and one of my fingers thinks." "That is very good," says the employer. Another man comes along, and says "he has two fingers that think." "Ah! that is better." But a third calls in and says that "all his fingers and thumbs think." That is better still. Finally another steps in and says, "I have a brain that thinks; I think all over; I am a thinking as well as a working man!" "You are the man I want," says the delighted employer.

Those men who have brains and experience are therefore the most valuable and not to be readily parted with; it is better for them, as well as yourself, to keep them, at reasonable advances in their salaries from time to time.

Don't Get Above Your Business

Young men after they get through their business training, or apprenticeship, instead of pursuing their avocation and rising in their business, will often lie about doing nothing. They say; "I have learned my business, but I am not going to be a hireling; what is the object of learning my trade or profession, unless I establish myself?'"

"Have you capital to start with?"

"No, but I am going to have it."

"How are you going to get it?"

"I will tell you confidentially; I have a wealthy old aunt, and she will die pretty soon; but if she does not, I expect to find some rich old man who will lend me a few thousands to give me a start. If I only get the money to start with I will do well."

There is no greater mistake than when a young man believes he will succeed with borrowed money. Why? Because every man's experience coincides with that of Mr. Astor, who said, "it was more difficult for him to accumulate his first thousand dollars, than all the succeeding millions that made up his colossal fortune." Money is good for nothing unless you know the value of it by experience. Give a boy twenty thousand dollars and put him in business, and the chances are that he will lose every dollar of it before he is a year older. Like buying a ticket in the lottery; and drawing a prize, it is "easy come, easy go." He does not know the value of it; nothing is worth anything, unless it costs effort. Without self-denial and economy; patience and perseverance, and commencing with capital which you have not earned, you are not sure to succeed in accumulating. Young men, instead of "waiting for dead men's shoes," should be up and doing, for there is no class of persons who are so unaccommodating in regard to dying as these rich old people, and it is fortunate for the expectant heirs that it is so. Nine out of ten of the rich men of our country to-day, started out in life as poor boys, with determined wills, industry, perseverance, economy and good habits. They went on gradually, made their own money and saved it; and this is the best way to acquire a fortune. Stephen Girard started life as a poor cabin boy, and died worth nine million dollars. A.T. Stewart was a poor Irish boy; and he paid taxes on a million and a half dollars of income, per year. John Jacob Astor was a poor farmer boy, and died worth twenty millions. Cornelius Vanderbilt began life rowing a boat from Staten Island to New York; he presented our government with a steamship worth a million of dollars, and died worth fifty million. "There is no royal road to learning," says the proverb, and I may say it is equally true, "there is no royal road to wealth." But I think there is a royal road to both. The road to learning is a royal one; the road that enables the student to expand his intellect and add every day to his stock of knowledge, until, in the pleasant process of intellectual growth, he is able to solve the most profound problems, to count the stars, to analyze every atom of the globe, and to measure the firmament this is a regal highway, and it is the only road worth traveling.

So in regard to wealth. Go on in confidence, study the rules, and above all things, study human nature; for "the proper study of mankind is man," and you will find that while expanding the intellect and the muscles, your enlarged experience will enable you every day to accumulate more and more principal, which will increase itself by interest and otherwise, until you arrive at a state of independence. You will find, as a general thing, that the poor boys get rich and the rich boys get poor. For instance, a rich man at his decease, leaves a large estate to his family. His eldest sons, who have helped him earn his fortune, know by experience the value of money; and they take their inheritance and add to it. The separate portions of the young children are placed at interest, and the little fellows are patted on the head, and told a dozen times a day, "you are rich; you will never have to work, you can always have whatever you wish, for you were born with a golden spoon in your mouth." The young heir soon finds out what that means;

he has the finest dresses and playthings; he is crammed with sugar candies and almost "killed with kindness," and he passes from school to school, petted and flattered. He becomes arrogant and self-conceited, abuses his teachers, and carries everything with a high hand. He knows nothing of the real value of money, having never earned any; but he knows all about the "golden spoon" business. At college, he invites his poor fellow-students to his room, where he "wines and dines" them. He is cajoled and caressed, and called a glorious good fellow, because he is so lavish of his money. He gives his game suppers, drives his fast horses, invites his chums to fetes and parties, determined to have lots of "good times." He spends the night in frolics and debauchery, and leads off his companions with the familiar song, "we won't go home till morning." He gets them to join him in pulling down signs, taking gates from their hinges and throwing them into back yards and horse-ponds. If the police arrest them, he knocks them down, is taken to the lockup, and joyfully foots the bills.

"Ah! my boys," he cries, "what is the use of being rich, if you can't enjoy yourself?"

He might more truly say, "if you can't make a fool of yourself;" but he is "fast," hates slow things, and doesn't "see it." Young men loaded down with other people's money are almost sure to lose all they inherit, and they acquire all sorts of bad habits which, in the majority of cases, ruin them in health, purse and character. In this country, one generation follows another, and the poor of to-day are rich in the next generation, or the third. Their experience leads them on, and they become rich, and they leave vast riches to their young children. These children, having been reared in luxury, are inexperienced and get poor; and after long experience another generation comes on and gathers up riches again in turn. And thus "history repeats itself," and happy is he who by listening to the experience of others avoids the rocks and shoals on which so many have been wrecked.

"In England, the business makes the man." If a man in that country is a mechanic or working-man, he is not recognized as a gentleman. On the occasion of my first appearance before Queen Victoria, the Duke of Wellington asked me what sphere in life General Tom Thumb's parents were in.

"His father is a carpenter," I replied.

"Oh! I had heard he was a gentleman," was the response of His Grace.

In this Republican country, the man makes the business. No matter whether he is a blacksmith, a shoemaker, a farmer, banker or lawyer, so long as his business is legitimate, he may be a gentleman. So any "legitimate" business is a double blessing it helps the man engaged in it, and also helps others. The Farmer supports his own family, but he also benefits the merchant or mechanic who needs the products of his farm. The tailor not only makes a living by his trade, but he also benefits the farmer, the clergyman and others who cannot make their own clothing. But all these classes often may be gentlemen.

The great ambition should be to excel all others engaged in the same occupation.

The college-student who was about graduating, said to an old lawyer:

"I have not yet decided which profession I will follow. Is your profession full?"

"The basement is much crowded, but there is plenty of room upstairs," was the witty and truthful reply.

No profession, trade, or calling, is overcrowded in the upper story. Wherever you find the most honest and intelligent merchant or banker, or the best lawyer, the best doctor, the best clergyman, the best shoemaker, carpenter, or anything else, that man is most sought for, and has always enough to do. As a nation, Americans are too superficial— they are striving to get rich quickly, and do not generally do their business as substantially and thoroughly as they should, but whoever excels all others in his own line, if his habits are good and his integrity undoubted, cannot fail to secure abundant patronage, and the wealth that naturally follows. Let your motto then always be "Excelsior," for by living up to it there is no such word as fail.

Learn Something Useful

Every man should make his son or daughter learn some useful trade or profession, so that in these days of changing fortunes of being rich to-day and poor tomorrow they may have something tangible to fall back upon. This provision might save many persons from misery, who by some unexpected turn of fortune have lost all their means.

Let Hope Predominate, but be not Too Visionary

Many persons are always kept poor, because they are too visionary. Every project looks to them like certain success, and therefore they keep changing from one business to another, always in hot water, always "under the harrow." The plan of "counting the chickens before they are hatched" is an error of ancient date, but it does not seem to improve by age.

Do not Scatter Your Powers

Engage in one kind of business only, and stick to it faithfully until you succeed, or until your experience shows that you should abandon it. A constant hammering on one nail will generally drive it home at last, so that it can be clinched. When a man's undivided attention is centered on one object, his mind will constantly be suggesting improvements of value, which would escape him if his brain was occupied by a dozen different subjects at once. Many a fortune has slipped through a man's fingers because he was engaged in too many occupations at a time. There is good sense in the old caution against having too many irons in the fire at once.

Be Systematic

Men should be systematic in their business. A person who does business by rule, having a time and place for everything, doing his work promptly, will accomplish twice as much and with half the trouble of him who does it carelessly and slipshod. By introducing system into all your transactions, doing one thing at a time, always meeting appointments with punctuality, you find leisure for pastime and recreation; whereas the man who only half does one thing, and then turns to something else, and half does that, will have his business at loose ends, and will never know when his day's work is done, for it never will be done. Of course, there is a limit to all these rules. We must try to preserve the happy medium, for there is such a thing as being too systematic. There are men and women, for instance, who put away things so carefully that they can never find them again. It is too much like the "red tape" formality at Washington, and Mr. Dickens' "Circumlocution Office,"—all theory and no result.

When the "Astor House" was first started in New York city, it was undoubtedly the best hotel in the country. The proprietors had learned a good deal in Europe regarding hotels, and the landlords were proud of the rigid system which pervaded every department of their great establishment. When twelve o'clock at night had arrived, and there were a number of guests around, one of the proprietors would say, "Touch that bell, John;" and in two minutes sixty servants, with a water-bucket in each hand, would present themselves in the hall. "This," said the landlord, addressing his guests, "is our fire-bell; it will show you we are quite safe here; we do everything systematically." This was before the

Croton water was introduced into the city. But they sometimes carried their system too far. On one occasion, when the hotel was thronged with guests, one of the waiters was suddenly indisposed, and although there were fifty waiters in the hotel, the landlord thought he must have his full complement, or his "system" would be interfered with. Just before dinner-time, he rushed down stairs and said, "There must be another waiter, I am one waiter short, what can I do?" He happened to see "Boots," the Irishman. "Pat," said he, "wash your hands and face; take that white apron and come into the dining-room in five minutes." Presently Pat appeared as required, and the proprietor said: "Now Pat, you must stand behind these two chairs, and wait on the gentlemen who will occupy them; did you ever act as a waiter?"

"I know all about it, sure, but I never did it."

Like the Irish pilot, on one occasion when the captain, thinking he was considerably out of his course, asked, "Are you certain you understand what you are doing?"

Pat replied, "Sure and I knows every rock in the channel."

That moment, "bang" thumped the vessel against a rock.

"Ah! be-jabers, and that is one of 'em," continued the pilot. But to return to the dining-room. "Pat," said the landlord, "here we do everything systematically. You must first give the gentlemen each a plate of soup, and when they finish that, ask them what they will have next."

Pat replied, "Ah! an' I understand parfectly the vartues of shystem."

Very soon in came the guests. The plates of soup were placed before them. One of Pat's two gentlemen ate his soup; the other did not care for it. He said: "Waiter, take this plate away and bring me some fish." Pat looked at the untasted plate of soup, and remembering the instructions of the landlord in regard to "system," replied: "Not till ye have ate yer supe!"

Of course that was carrying "system" entirely too far.

Read the Newspapers

Always take a trustworthy newspaper, and thus keep thoroughly posted in regard to the transactions of the world. He who is without a newspaper is cut off from his species. In these days of telegraphs and steam, many important inventions and improvements in every branch of trade are being made, and he who don't consult the newspapers will soon find himself and his business left out in the cold.

Beware of "Outside Operations"

We sometimes see men who have obtained fortunes, suddenly become poor. In many cases, this arises from intemperance, and often from gaming, and other bad habits. Frequently it occurs because a man has been engaged in "outside operations," of some sort. When he gets rich in his legitimate business, he is told of a grand speculation where he can make a score of thousands. He is constantly flattered by his friends, who tell him that he is born lucky, that everything he touches turns into gold. Now if he forgets that his economical habits, his rectitude of conduct and a personal attention to a business which he understood, caused his success in life, he will listen to the siren voices. He says:

"I will put in twenty thousand dollars. I have been lucky, and my good luck will soon bring me back sixty thousand dollars."

A few days elapse and it is discovered he must put in ten thousand dollars more: soon after he is told "it is all right," but certain matters not foreseen, require an advance of twenty thousand dollars more, which will bring him a rich harvest; but before the time comes around to realize, the bubble bursts, he loses all he is possessed of, and then he learns what he ought to have known at the first, that however successful a man may be in his own business, if he turns from that and engages ill a business which he don't understand, he is like Samson when shorn of his locks his strength has departed, and he becomes like other men.

If a man has plenty of money, he ought to invest something in everything that appears to promise success, and that will probably benefit mankind; but let the sums thus invested be moderate in amount, and never let a man foolishly jeopardize a fortune that he has earned in a legitimate way, by investing it in things in which he has had no experience.

Don't Indorse without Security

I hold that no man ought ever to indorse a note or become security, for any man, be it his father or brother, to a greater extent than he can afford to lose and care nothing about, without taking good security. Here is a man that is worth twenty thousand dollars; he is doing a thriving manufacturing or mercantile trade; you are retired and living on your money; he comes to you and says:

"You are aware that I am worth twenty thousand dollars, and don't owe a dollar; if I had five thousand dollars in cash, I could purchase a particular lot of goods and double my money in a couple of months; will you indorse my note for that amount?"

You reflect that he is worth twenty thousand dollars, and you incur no risk by endorsing his note; you like to accommodate him, and you lend your name without taking the precaution of getting security. Shortly after, he shows you the note with your endorsement canceled, and tells you, probably truly, "that he made the profit that he expected by the operation," you reflect that you have done a good action, and the thought makes you feel happy. By and by, the same thing occurs again and you do it again; you have already fixed the impression in your mind that it is perfectly safe to indorse his notes without security.

But the trouble is, this man is getting money too easily. He has only to take your note to the bank, get it discounted and take the cash. He gets money for the time being without effort; without inconvenience to himself. Now mark the result. He sees a chance for speculation outside of his business. A temporary investment of only $10,000 is required. It is sure to come back before a note at the bank would be due. He places a note for that amount before you. You sign it almost mechanically. Being firmly convinced that your friend is responsible and trustworthy; you indorse his notes as a "matter of course."

Unfortunately the speculation does not come to a head quite so soon as was expected, and another $10,000 note must be discounted to take up the last one when due. Before this note matures the speculation has proved an utter failure and all the money is lost. Does the loser tell his friend, the endorser, that he has lost half of his fortune? Not at all. He don't even mention that he has speculated at all. But he has got excited; the spirit of speculation has seized him; he sees others making large sums in this way (we seldom hear of the losers), and, like other speculators, he "looks for his money where he loses it." He tries again. endorsing notes has become chronic with you, and at every loss he gets your signature for whatever amount he wants. Finally you discover your friend has lost all of his property and all of yours. You are overwhelmed with astonishment and grief, and you say "it is a hard thing; my friend here has ruined me," but, you should add, "I have also ruined him." If you had said in the first place, "I will accommodate you, but I never indorse without taking ample security," he could not have gone beyond the length of his tether, and he would never have been tempted away from his legitimate business. It is a very dangerous thing, therefore, at any time, to let people get possession of money too easily; it tempts them to hazardous speculations, if nothing more. Solomon truly said "he that hateth suretiship is sure."

So with the young man starting in business; let him understand the value of money by earning it. When he does understand its value, then grease the wheels a little in helping him to start business, but remember, men who get money with too great facility cannot usually succeed. You must get the first dollars by hard knocks, and at some sacrifice, in order to appreciate the value of those dollars.

Advertise Your Business

We all depend, more or less, upon the public for our support. We all trade with the public—lawyers, doctors, shoemakers, artists, blacksmiths, showmen, opera stagers, railroad presidents, and college professors. Those who deal with the public must be careful that their goods are valuable; that they are genuine, and will give satisfaction. When you get an article which you know is going to please your customers, and that when they have tried it, they will feel they have got their money's worth, then let the fact be known that you have got it. Be careful to advertise it in some shape or other because it is evident that if a man has ever so good an article for sale, and nobody knows it, it will bring him no return. In a country like this, where nearly everybody reads, and where newspapers are issued and circulated in editions of five thousand to two hundred thousand, it would be very unwise if this channel was not taken advantage of to reach the public in advertising. A newspaper goes into the family, and is read by wife and children, as well as the head of the home; hence hundreds and thousands of people may read your advertisement, while you are attending to your routine business. Many, perhaps, read it while you are asleep. The whole philosophy of life is, first "sow," then "reap." That is the way the farmer does; he plants his potatoes and corn, and sows his grain, and then goes about something else, and the time comes when he reaps. But he never reaps first and sows afterwards. This principle applies to all kinds of business, and to nothing more eminently than to advertising. If a man has a genuine article, there is no way in which he can reap more advantageously than by "sowing" to the public in this way. He must, of course, have a really good article, and one which will please his customers; anything spurious will not succeed permanently because the public is wiser than many imagine. Men and women are selfish, and we all prefer purchasing where we can get the most for our money and we try to find out where we can most surely do so.

You may advertise a spurious article, and induce many people to call and buy it once, but they will denounce you as an impostor and swindler, and your business will gradually die out and leave you poor. This is right. Few people can safely depend upon chance custom. You all need to have your customers return and purchase again. A man said to me, "I have tried advertising and did not succeed; yet I have a good article."

I replied, "My friend, there may be exceptions to a general rule. But how do you advertise?"

"I put it in a weekly newspaper three times, and paid a dollar and a half for it." I replied: "Sir, advertising is like learning—'a little is a dangerous thing!'"

A French writer says that "The reader of a newspaper does not see the first mention of an ordinary advertisement; the second insertion he sees, but does not read; the third insertion he reads; the fourth insertion, he looks at the price; the fifth insertion, he speaks of it to his wife; the sixth insertion, he is ready to purchase, and the seventh insertion, he purchases." Your object in advertising is to make the public understand what you have got to sell, and if you have not the pluck to keep advertising, until you have imparted that information, all the money you have spent is lost. You are like the fellow who told the gentleman if he would give him ten cents it would save him a dollar. "How can I help you so much with so small a sum?" asked the gentleman in surprise. "I started out this morning (hiccuped the fellow) with the full determination to get drunk, and I have spent my only dollar to accomplish the object, and it has not quite done it. Ten cents worth more of whiskey would just do it, and in this manner I should save the dollar already expended."

So a man who advertises at all must keep it up until the public know who and what he is, and what his business is, or else the money invested in advertising is lost.

Some men have a peculiar genius for writing a striking advertisement, one that will arrest the attention of the reader at first sight. This fact, of course, gives the advertiser a great advantage. Sometimes a man makes himself popular by an unique sign or a curious display in his window, recently I observed a swing sign extending over the sidewalk in front of a store, on which was the inscription in plain letters,

"Don't Read the Other Side"

Of course I did, and so did everybody else, and I learned that the man had made all independence by first attracting the public to his business in that way and then using his customers well afterwards.

Genin, the hatter, bought the first Jenny Lind ticket at auction for two hundred and twenty-five dollars, because he knew it would be a good advertisement for him. "Who is the bidder?" said the auctioneer, as he knocked down that ticket at Castle Garden. "Genin, the hatter," was the response. Here were thousands of people from the Fifth avenue, and from distant cities in the highest stations in life. "Who is 'Genin,' the hatter?" they exclaimed. They had never heard of him before. The next morning the newspapers and telegraph had circulated the facts from Maine to Texas, and from five to ten millions off people had read that the tickets sold at auction For Jenny Lind's first concert amounted to about twenty thousand dollars, and that a single ticket was sold at two hundred and twenty-five dollars, to "Genin, the hatter." Men throughout the country involuntarily took off their hats to see if they had a "Genin" hat on their heads. At a town in Iowa it was found that in the crowd around the post office, there was one man who had a "Genin" hat, and he showed it in triumph, although it was worn out and not worth two cents. "Why," one man exclaimed, "you have a real 'Genin' hat; what a lucky fellow you are." Another man said, "Hang on to that hat, it will be a valuable heir-loom in your family." Still another man in the crowd who seemed to envy the possessor of this good fortune, said, "Come, give us all a chance; put it up at auction!" He did so, and it was sold as a keepsake for nine dollars and fifty cents! What was the consequence to Mr. Genin? He sold ten thousand extra hats per annum, the first six years. Nine-tenths of the purchasers bought of him, probably, out of curiosity, and many of them, finding that he gave them an equivalent for their money, became his regular customers. This novel advertisement first struck their attention, and then, as he made a good article, they came again.

Now I don't say that everybody should advertise as Mr. Genin did. But I say if a man has got goods for sale, and he don't advertise them in some way, the chances are that some day the sheriff will do it for him. Nor do I say that everybody must advertise in a newspaper, or indeed use "printers' ink" at all. On the contrary, although that article is indispensable in the majority of cases, yet doctors and clergymen, and sometimes lawyers and some others, can more effectually reach the public in some other manner. But it is obvious, they must be known in some way, else how could they be supported?

Be Polite and Kind to Your Customers

Politeness and civility are the best capital ever invested in business. Large stores, gilt signs, flaming advertisements, will all prove unavailing if you or your employees treat your patrons abruptly. The truth is, the more kind and liberal a man is, the more generous will be the patronage bestowed upon him. "Like begets like." The man who gives the greatest amount of goods of a corresponding quality for the least sum (still reserving for himself a profit) will generally succeed best in the long run. This brings us to the golden rule, "As ye would that men should do to you, do ye also to them" and they will do better by you than if you always treated them as if you wanted to get the most you could out of them for the least return. Men who drive sharp bargains with their customers, acting as if they never expected to see them again, will not be mistaken. They will never see them again as customers. People don't like to pay and get kicked also.

One of the ushers in my Museum once told me he intended to whip a man who was in the lecture-room as soon as he came out.

"What for?" I inquired.

"Because he said I was no gentleman," replied the usher.

"Never mind," I replied, "he pays for that, and you will not convince him you are a gentleman by whipping him. I cannot afford to lose a customer. If you whip him, he will never visit the Museum again, and he will induce friends to go with him to other places of amusement instead of this, and thus you see, I should be a serious loser."

"But he insulted me," muttered the usher.

"Exactly," I replied, "and if he owned the Museum, and you had paid him for the privilege of visiting it, and he had then insulted you, there might be some reason in your resenting it, but in this instance he is the man who pays, while we receive, and you must, therefore, put up with his bad manners."

My usher laughingly remarked, that this was undoubtedly the true policy; but he added that he should not object to an increase of salary if he was expected to be abused in order to promote my interest.

Be Charitable

Of course men should be charitable, because it is a duty and a pleasure. But even as a matter of policy, if you possess no higher incentive, you will find that the liberal man will command patronage, while the sordid, uncharitable miser will be avoided.

Solomon says: "There is that scattereth and yet increaseth; and there is that withholdeth more than meet, but it tendeth to poverty." Of course the only true charity is that which is from the heart.

The best kind of charity is to help those who are willing to help themselves. Promiscuous almsgiving, without inquiring into the worthiness of the applicant, is bad in every sense. But to search out and quietly assist those who are struggling for themselves, is the kind that "scattereth and yet increaseth." But don't fall into the idea that some persons practice, of giving a prayer instead of a potato, and a benediction instead of bread, to the hungry. It is easier to make Christians with full stomachs than empty.

Don't Blab

Some men have a foolish habit of telling their business secrets. If they make money they like to tell their neighbors how it was done. Nothing is gained by this, and ofttimes much is lost. Say nothing about your profits, your hopes, your expectations, your intentions. And this should apply to letters as well as to conversation. Goethe makes Mephistophilles say: "Never write a letter nor destroy one." Business men must write letters, but they should be careful what they put in them. If you are losing money, be specially cautious and not tell of it, or you will lose your reputation.

Preserve Your Integrity

It is more precious than diamonds or rubies. The old miser said to his sons: "Get money; get it honestly if you can, but get money:" This advice was not only atrociously wicked, but it was the very essence of stupidity: It was as much as to say, "if you find it difficult to obtain money honestly, you can easily get it dishonestly. Get it in that way." Poor fool! Not to know that the most difficult thing in life is to make money dishonestly! Not to know that our prisons are full of men who attempted to follow this advice; not to understand that no man can be dishonest, without soon being found out, and that when his lack of principle is discovered, nearly every avenue to success is closed against him forever. The public very properly shun all whose integrity is doubted. No matter how polite and pleasant and accommodating a man may be, none of us dare to deal with him if we suspect "false weights and measures." Strict honesty, not only lies at the foundation of all success in life (financially), but in every other respect. Uncompromising integrity of character is invaluable. It secures to its possessor a peace and joy which cannot be attained without it—which no amount of money, or houses and lands can purchase. A man who is known to be strictly honest, may be ever so poor, but he has the purses of all the community at his disposal—for all know that if he promises to return what he borrows, he will never disappoint them. As a mere matter of selfishness, therefore, if a man had no higher motive for being honest, all will find that the maxim of Dr. Franklin can never fail to be true, that "honesty is the best policy."

To get rich, is not always equivalent to being successful. "There are many rich poor men," while there are many others, honest and devout men and women, who have never possessed so much money as some rich persons squander in a week, but who are nevertheless really richer and happier than any man can ever be while he is a transgressor of the higher laws of his being.

The inordinate love of money, no doubt, may be and is "the root of all evil," but money itself, when properly used, is not only a "handy thing to have in the house," but affords the gratification of blessing our race by enabling its possessor to enlarge the scope of human happiness and human influence. The desire for wealth is nearly universal, and none can say it is not laudable, provided the possessor of it accepts its responsibilities, and uses it as a friend to humanity.

The history of money-getting, which is commerce, is a history of civilization, and wherever trade has flourished most, there, too, have art and science produced the noblest fruits. In fact, as a general thing, money-getters are the benefactors of our race. To them, in a great measure, are we indebted for our institutions of learning and of art, our academies, colleges and churches. It is no argument against the desire for, or the possession of wealth, to say that there are sometimes misers who hoard money only for the sake of hoarding and who have no higher aspiration than to grasp everything which comes within their reach. As we have sometimes hypocrites in religion, and demagogues in politics, so there are occasionally misers among money-getters. These, however, are only exceptions to the general rule. But when, in this country, we find such a nuisance and stumbling block as a miser, we remember with gratitude that in America we have no laws of primogeniture, and that in the due course of nature the time will come when the hoarded dust will be scattered for the benefit of mankind. To all men and women, therefore, do I conscientiously say, make money honestly, and not otherwise, for Shakespeare has truly said, "He that wants money, means, and content, is without three good friends."

www.ingramcontent.com/pod-product-compliance
Lightning Source LLC
LaVergne TN
LVHW020426070526
838199LV00004B/297